Mountain Mist® Quilt Favorites

"For the winter I think I shall make a quilt to keep from getting lonesome, for some of the women around here are real interested in quilting again."
Minnesota letter, 1931

Oxmoor House®

Mountain Mist Quilt Favorites
from the *For the Love of Quilting* series
©1998 by Oxmoor House, Inc.
Book Division of Southern Progress Corporation
P.O. Box 2463, Birmingham, Alabama 35201

Published by Oxmoor House, Inc., and Leisure Arts, Inc.

Library of Congress Catalog Card Number: 97-75544
Hardcover ISBN: 0-8487-1668-X
Softcover ISBN: 0-8487-1669-8
Manufactured in the United States of America
First Printing 1998

Editor-in-Chief: Nancy Fitzpatrick Wyatt
Senior Crafts Editor: Susan Ramey Cleveland
Senior Editor, Editorial Services: Olivia K. Wells
Art Director: James Boone

Mountain Mist Quilt Favorites
Editor: Patricia Wilens
Copy Editor: Susan S. Cheatham
Associate Art Director: Cynthia R. Cooper
Designer: Alison Turner Bachofer
Illustrator: Kelly Davis
Senior Photographer: John O'Hagan
Photo Stylist: Linda Baltzell Wright
Production Director: Phillip Lee
Associate Production Manager: Theresa L. Beste
Production Assistant: Faye Porter Bonner

We're Here For You!
Oxmoor House is dedicated to serving you with reliable
information that expands your imagination and enriches
your life. We welcome your comments and suggestions.
Please write us at:

Oxmoor House
Editor, *Mountain Mist Quilt Favorites*
2100 Lakeshore Drive
Birmingham, AL 35209

To order additional publications, including *Quilter's Complete
Guide*, please call 1-205-877-6560.

Contents

Introduction

The Grace of Appliqué

Pomegranate, page 63

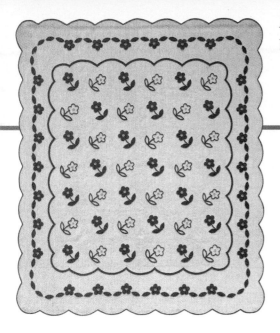

Forget-Me-Not, page 68

Shadow Trail, page 106

The Pleasures of Patchwork

General Instructions

The Story of Mountain Mist® Patterns

"There are many reasons why the art of quiltmaking has lasted so long and why it is going to continue . . . for generations to come. As a recreation to calm overwrought nerves of our day and age, there is nothing like quilting . . . Then, too, what can be more fulfilling than creating something beautiful?"

Phoebe Edwards, 1938

In most respects, the 1930s were hard times. The United States was gripped by the economic gloom of the Great Depression. World war was brewing overseas. But now we look back at those years as a golden age of American quiltmaking.

Throughout the 1930s, quiltmaking captured a lot of attention. In 1933, a Detroit exhibit of Mountain Mist® quilts attracted more than 50,000 people in just three days. In a time of dust bowls and bread lines, why did so many take up quilting? Answers are found in the fashions of the day, seasoned with the marketing savvy of manufacturers of products like Mountain Mist batting. And, as Phoebe Edwards said, a hunger to create something beautiful.

The Colonial Revival
In the late 1800s, quiltmaking was at a low ebb. Victorian trend-setters such as *Godey's Lady's Book* sneered at homemade quilts as "unhealthy" and unstylish. Attitudes started to change just before the turn of the century with the Arts and Crafts movement, which idealized folk arts and handwork.

The roaring 1920s were years of peace, prosperity, and national pride—the calm

before the storm. The new woman turned her back on Victorian styles of dress and decorating. The U.S. had saved Europe in the Great War and all things American were in vogue. Experts now decreed that Early American-style beds and bedding were "built for a new service and a new conception of hygiene."

Pastel and floral Depression-era quilts are a product of the happy 1920s. When hard times hit, few could afford such quilts, but perhaps the emotional need was greater. People craved what quilt historian Merikay Waldvogel calls "soft covers for hard times."

The Quilting Bandwagon
This nationwide conformity of styles, colors, and patterns was fueled by something new—national marketing and advertising that established a standard of style and taste. Unlike Victorian magazines, new periodicals had photographs to show the reader what was recommended. No longer was it necessary for imagination to fill in the blanks.

In her 1915 book *Quilts: Their Story and How to Make Them*, Marie Webster touted quiltmaking as an activity that would keep "the family hearth flame bright." Webster,

"Women are quilting when they formerly went out stepping."

Chicago *Daily News*, 1933

Stacks of Mountain Mist batting provide a backdrop for this 1933 department store quilting demonstration. Exhibits and displays such as this fueled the popularity of quilting in the 1920s and 1930s.

needlework editor at *Ladies' Home Journal* from 1911 to 1917, was one of the first to sell mail-order quilt patterns. Her stylish designs reflected the art nouveau and "Early American" trends of the day. Others who sold mail-order quilt patterns were Anne Orr of Nashville (needlework editor at *Good Housekeeping* from 1919 to 1940) and Mrs. Scioto Danner of El Dorado, Kansas.

Newspapers like The Kansas City *Star* found quilting columns to be popular features. In 1933, the Chicago *Daily News* noted that women were quilting "when they formerly went out stepping." Even periodicals like *Progressive Farmer* included quilt patterns between reports on corn and cattle.

By the mid-1920s, quilting was a mass-marketed national fad. The textile industry provided abundant low-cost cotton fabrics in the clear pastel colors that typify Depression-era quilts. By the time of the stock market crash in 1929, mail-order merchandising brought consumer goods to the most isolated corners of the nation. *continued*

Meet Phoebe Edwards

Phoebe Lloyd used her grandmother's maiden name, Edwards, in her role as the public voice of Mountain Mist. From 1929 to 1937, Phoebe worked on more than 50 patterns, creating original designs and styling others, working with the ladies who made many of the quilts shown in this book. Dispensing advice to customers by mail, in magazine articles, and in newspaper columns, "Phoebe Edwards" became so well-known that Phoebe bequeathed the name to the company when she left. Since then, several people haved filled in as "Phoebe Edwards" to serve consumers. The original Phoebe's signature still appears on batting packaging with the customer-help telephone number.

Mountain Mist batting labels from the 1930s feature drawings of available free patterns. The Lone Star pattern shown, dated 1935, includes a packet of fabric swatches for the quilt shown on page 141.

Pattern Popularity

Mountain Mist patterns were a great success. To make them even more attractive to consumers, the wrapper included a coupon that the quilter could use to order another pattern for 20 cents. Just three years after the promotion began, Stearns & Foster was selling more than 55,500 patterns a year above and beyond the patterns given free with a batting purchase.

Mountain Mist quilts were springing up everywhere, winning prizes at state and local fairs. Quiltmakers entered more than 24,000 quilts in the 1933 Sears National Quilt Contest, and several of the 30 finalists were Mountain Mist patterns.

Let's Put on a Show!

Local quilt shows and contests were an important element in the marketing strategy of companies like Stearns & Foster. In a time when cost-free entertainment was scarce, it's no wonder quilt shows drew big crowds. A two-week quilt show at Macy's department store had sophisticated New Yorkers lined up for hours to see the exhibit.

The Mountain Mist Historical Collection of quilts featured in this book began as a marketing tool for such shows. In 1934, a St. Louis store manager wrote to Stearns & Foster, "We are more than pleased with the results of this quilt show. We have sold more Mountain Mist batts in two weeks than we have sold for the past six months."

> "There is a thrill when you finish the quilt top and stand off to admire your handiwork . . . you are filled with pride."
>
> Phoebe Edwards, 1938

Stars of Alabama, page 126

Mountain Mist Wraps Up Business

Batting manufacturers at Cincinnati's Stearns & Foster Co. saw that there was profit to be made in quiltmaking. In 1929, a sales manager came up with an idea that would boost sales of the newly named Mountain Mist brand of cotton batting.

Frederick J. Hooker's idea was to print a pattern and instructions on the inside of each colorful paper wrapper. Since quilting is nearly the last step in making a quilt, giving a pattern with the batt could encourage the quilter to start another project.

The first Mountain Mist patterns were 20 time-honored classics and original designs such as *Tumbling Blocks* and *Windblow Tulip.* A new batting package featured color illustrations of blocks and a distinctive red, white, and blue *Tumbling Blocks* border that identifies Mountain Mist products to this day.

Hooker interviewed quilters in Kentucky, Tennessee, and Ohio, buying antique quilts on which Mountain Mist patterns were based. These were the beginning of Mountain Mist's collection of historical quilts, which is featured in this book.

Chanticleer, page 46

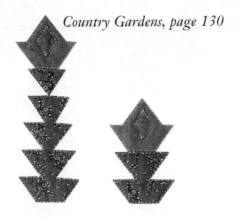

Country Gardens, page 130

Stearns & Foster helped retailers stage their own shows and contests with equal success. A planner, ready-made newspaper ads, statement enclosures, and display cards were among the support materials offered by Mountain Mist for local shows. King's Dry Goods in Kearney, Nebraska, reported the biggest yard-goods sales in its history when it staged a quilt show in 1933.

Blue Book Value

The Mountain Mist Blue Book of Quilt Patterns was an important sales support tool that started in the mid-1930s and continues today. The Blue Book shows consumers drawings or photos of available patterns and ordering information. Information on ordering the current Mountain Mist Blue Book is on page 73.

Changing the Names

Stearns & Foster, like other mail-order companies, often assigned new names to updated patterns. This contributed to the loss of traditional regional names, as quilters accepted the mass-marketed version.

For example, *New York Beauty* was called *Rocky Mountain Road* or *Crown of Thorns* in the 1800s. But the popularity of Mountain Mist's patterns prevailed over the old names.

Changing Times

After a decline in quiltmaking during World War II and the 1950s, quiltmaking began yet another revival in the 1970s. The Whitney Museum in New York staged an exhibit of antique quilts in 1971, and suddenly quilts were hot as an art form. Books and magazines continue to feed the desire for new quilts and quiltmaking techniques.

Mountain Mist continued to include free patterns with each batt until the advent of plastic wrappers in the 1970s. Most of the 130 patterns are still available (see page 73), ripe for new interpretations in today's fabrics.

Mountain Mist patterns are the quilts that our grandmothers loved. This book offers a sampling of these quilts with revised instructions to reflect today's new methods. Make these old favorites into new classics that will be appreciated for generations to come.

Bibliography

Waldvogel, Merikay. *Soft Covers for Hard Times: Quiltmaking & the Great Depression.* Nashville, TN: Rutledge Hill Press, 1990. ISBN 1-55853-062-2.

Woodard, Thos. K., and Blanche Greenstein. *Twentieth Century Quilts.* New York: E.P. Dutton, 1988. ISBN 0-525-48115-X.

Boston Commons, page 97

The Grace of Appliqué

"A revival of patchwork quilts is at hand, and dainty fingers . . . are busy placing the blocks together in new and artistic patterns, as well as in the real old-time order."

Ladies' Home Journal, October 1894

Windblown Tulip

Hollyhocks

This pattern, copyrighted by Mountain Mist in 1934, was adapted from a design by Mrs. Frank H. Trapp of Taylorville, Illinois. Quilting in the setting blocks repeats the hollyhocks design.

Finished Size: 73" x 92"

Materials

6½ yards yellow
2⅝ yards dark blue
2 yards white
1 yard green
⅝ yard light blue
⅜ yard medium pink
¼ yard *each* of light pink, dark pink, medium purple, dark purple, medium orange, and dark orange
⅛ yard (or scraps) *each* of light purple and light orange
5½ yards backing fabric
81" x 96" precut batting
Tracing paper and pencil

Cutting

Make templates for stem and patterns A–K on pages 12, 14, and 15. Add seam allowances to appliqués when cutting. Cut pieces in order listed to make best use of yardage.

From yellow, cut:
- 16 (9½" x 11½") side blocks.
- 24 (9½") setting squares.
- 88 of Pattern D.

From dark blue, cut:
- 4 (2½" x 90") lengthwise strips for outer borders.
- 33" square for binding.
- 8 (5½" x 10½") pieces for appliqué rows.
- 12 (1½" x 33") strips for sashing.

From white, cut:
- 4 (5½" x 68½") lengthwise strips for appliqué rows.
- 8 of Pattern B.

From green, cut:
- 11 (1¼" x 42") cross-grain strips for stems. See appliqué instructions, Step 2, to cut stems from pattern.
- 32 of Pattern A.
- 16 of Pattern E.
- 8 of Pattern E reversed.
- 28 of Pattern H.
- 20 of Pattern I.
- 40 of Pattern K.

From light blue, cut:
- 12 (1½" x 32") strips for sashing.

From medium pink, cut:
- 4 of Pattern B.
- 16 of Pattern C.
- 12 of Pattern G.

From light pink, cut:
- 4 of Pattern B.
- 4 of Pattern F.
- 12 of Pattern C.

From dark pink, cut:
- 4 of Pattern C.
- 24 of Pattern F.
- 16 of Pattern J.

From *each* of light purple and light orange, cut:
- 2 of Pattern B.
- 6 of Pattern C.
- 2 of Pattern F.

From *each* of medium purple and medium orange, cut:
- 2 of Pattern B.
- 10 of Pattern C.
- 8 of Pattern G.

From *each* of dark purple and dark orange, cut:
- 2 of Pattern C.
- 16 of Pattern F.
- 12 of Pattern J.

continued

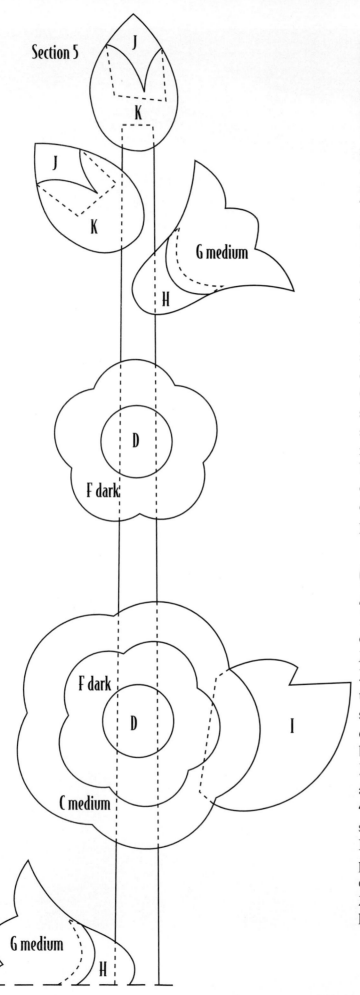

Section 5

J

K

J

K

G medium

H

D

F dark

F dark

D

I

C medium

G medium

H

Making a Pattern

Appliqué is easier if you work with a complete tracing of the design. When appliqué is complete, save the pattern to use later to make a quilting stencil.

1. Tape 5"-wide pieces of tracing paper together to make a paper rectangle 42" long.

2. Center paper over Section 1 pattern on page 14, aligning end of paper strip with bottom of stem. Trace pattern. Include markings for underlap on each group of leaves and flowers.

3. Center paper strip over Section 2 pattern on page 14, aligning Section 1 drawing with overlap indicated on pattern. Trace Section 2.

4. Continue tracing sections 3, 4, and 5 in this manner to complete pattern.

5. Make a separate tracing of Section 5 only for side appliqué blocks, eliminating G/H flower at bottom of stem.

6. Use complete pattern to position pieces on each strip using one of the following methods:

a) center fabric strip on pattern and use a nonpermanent marker to *lightly* trace design on fabric;

b) tape pattern to a windowpane; then tape fabric over it and pin appliqué pieces in place;

c) center pattern over fabric and slide appliqués into position under it, pinning pieces in place.

Center Appliqué Rows

See Quilt Smart Workshop, page 157, for tips on appliqué.

1. Sew a 5½" x 10½" dark blue piece to both ends of each white strip to get a pieced strip 88½" long. Make 4 for appliqué rows.

2. From complete traced pattern, make a paper pattern for long stem. Adding seam allowance on all sides, cut 8 stems from green strips. Turn under side edges only; it is not necessary to turn under top and bottom edges.

3. Align bottom edge of each stem with an end of an appliqué row and pin in place.

4. Referring to Making a Pattern, Step 6, use chosen method to pin flowers and leaves on each stem. Refer to patterns at left and on pages 14 and 15 for placement of light, medium, and dark fabrics for each stalk. Referring to photo on page 11, notice that 2 rows have pink flowers at both ends and 2 rows have a purple stalk opposite an orange stalk.

5. When satisfied with position of pieces on each stalk, appliqué stems, leaves, and flowers. Start stitching at bottom of each stalk and work up to its top. Pin overlapping pieces out of the way to stitch stems and leaves in place.
6. Appliqué 4 rows.

Side Block Appliqué

1. Use Section 5 tracing to make a paper pattern for short stems. Adding seam allowance on all sides, cut 12 stems from remaining green strips. Turn under side edges only.
2. Align bottom of each stem with an edge of each 9½" x 11½" yellow block. Pin in place.
3. Pin leaves and flowers on each stem to make 4 each of orange, pink, and purple stalks. Refer to pattern on page 12 for placement of light, medium, and dark fabrics for each color.
4. When satisfied with placement, stitch pieces in place.
5. Appliqué 12 side blocks.

Making Sashing

1. Join light blue and dark blue strips as shown (**Strip Set Diagram**). Make 12 strip sets. Press seam allowances toward dark blue.
2. Cut 14 (11½"-wide) segments, cutting at least 1 segment from each strip set. From remaining strip sets, cut 21 (9½"-wide) segments for sashing.

Strip Set Diagram

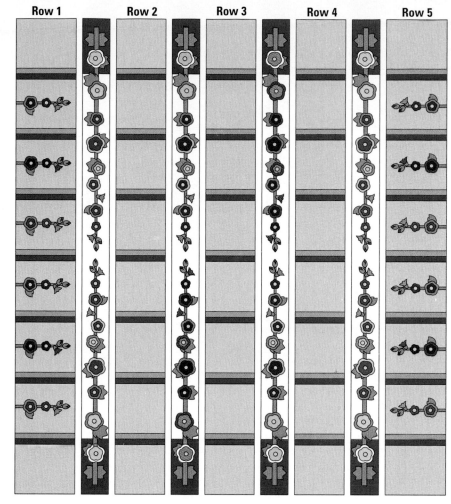

Row 1   Row 2   Row 3   Row 4   Row 5

Quilt Assembly Diagram

Quilt Assembly

Refer to photo and Quilt Assembly Diagram *throughout.*
1. For Row 1, select 6 appliquéd side blocks (2 of each color), 2 plain side blocks, and 7 (11½"-wide) sashing strips. Arrange units as shown. Repeat for Row 5.
2. For *each* of rows 2, 3, and 4, select 8 setting squares and 7 (9½"-wide) sashing strips. Arrange units as shown.
3. Join blocks in each row. Press seams away from sashing.
4. Place appliquéd rows between pieced rows. Check position of rows; then join rows as shown.

Borders

1. Measure length of quilt; then trim 2 borders to match quilt length. Sew borders to quilt sides. Press seams toward borders.
2. Measure width of quilt and trim remaining borders to match quilt width. Sew borders to top and bottom edges of quilt.

Quilting and Finishing

1. Mark quilting design on quilt top as desired. To quilt your quilt top as shown, make a stencil of paper pattern. Or, if you prefer, position quilt top over drawing and trace design. Mark hollyhock stalks in setting squares, parallel

continued

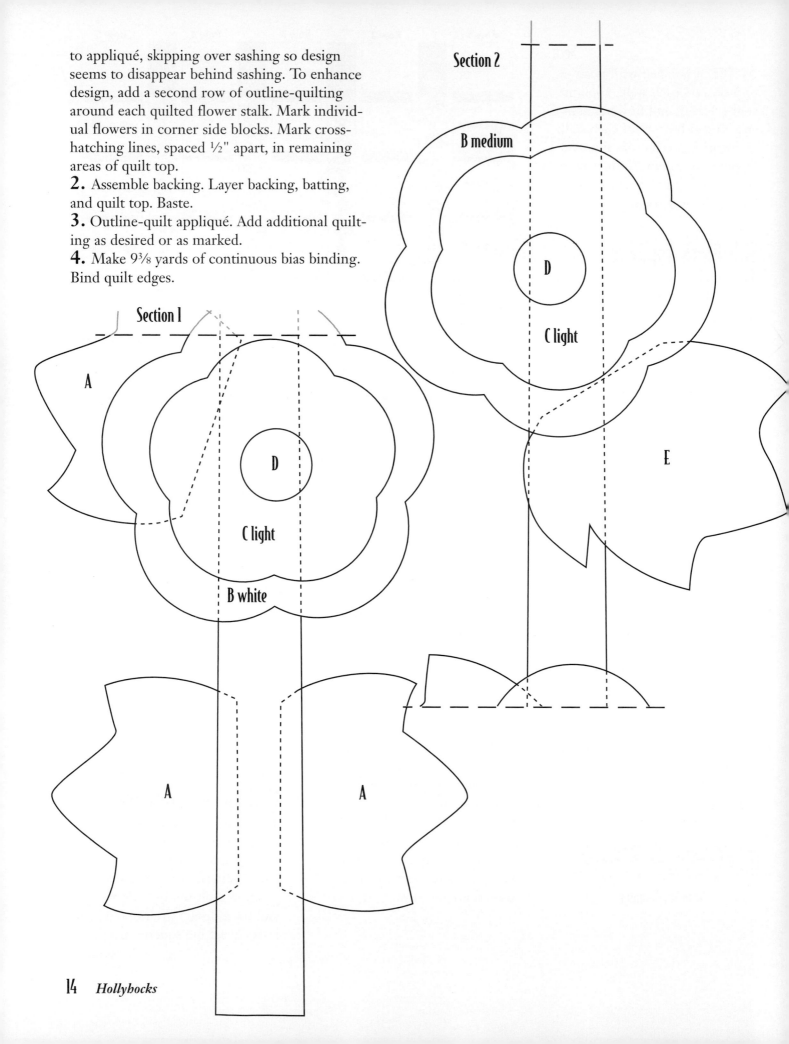

to appliqué, skipping over sashing so design seems to disappear behind sashing. To enhance design, add a second row of outline-quilting around each quilted flower stalk. Mark individual flowers in corner side blocks. Mark cross-hatching lines, spaced ½" apart, in remaining areas of quilt top.

2. Assemble backing. Layer backing, batting, and quilt top. Baste.

3. Outline-quilt appliqué. Add additional quilting as desired or as marked.

4. Make 9⅜ yards of continuous bias binding. Bind quilt edges.

Section 2

B medium

D

C light

E

Section 1

A

D

C light

B white

A

A

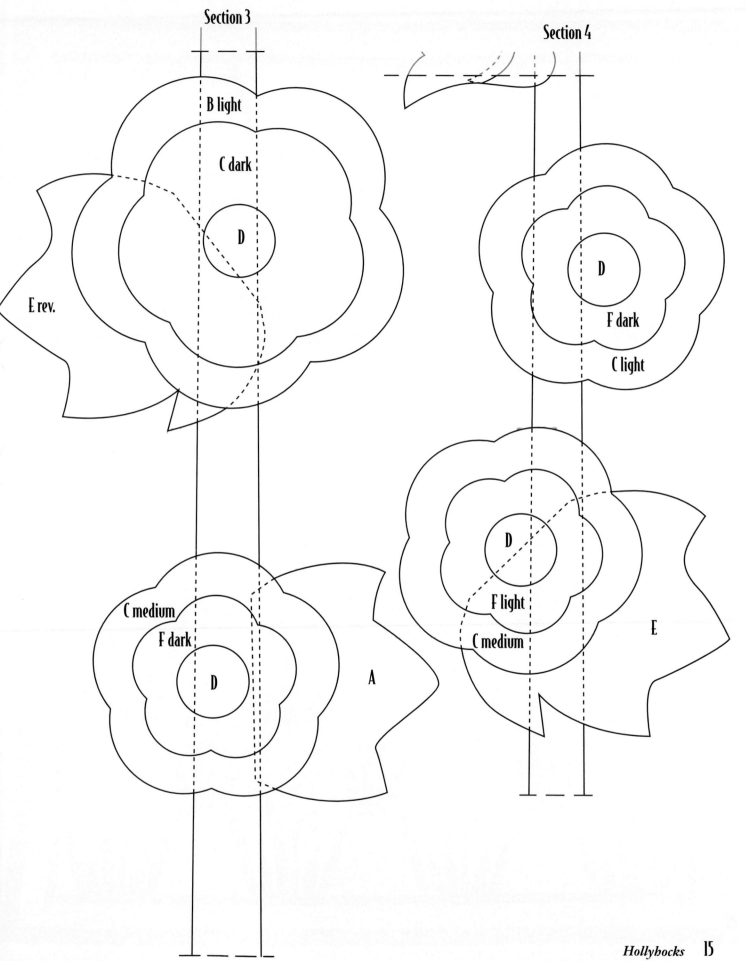

Section 3

B light

C dark

D

E rev.

C medium

F dark

D

A

Section 4

D

F dark

C light

D

F light

C medium

E

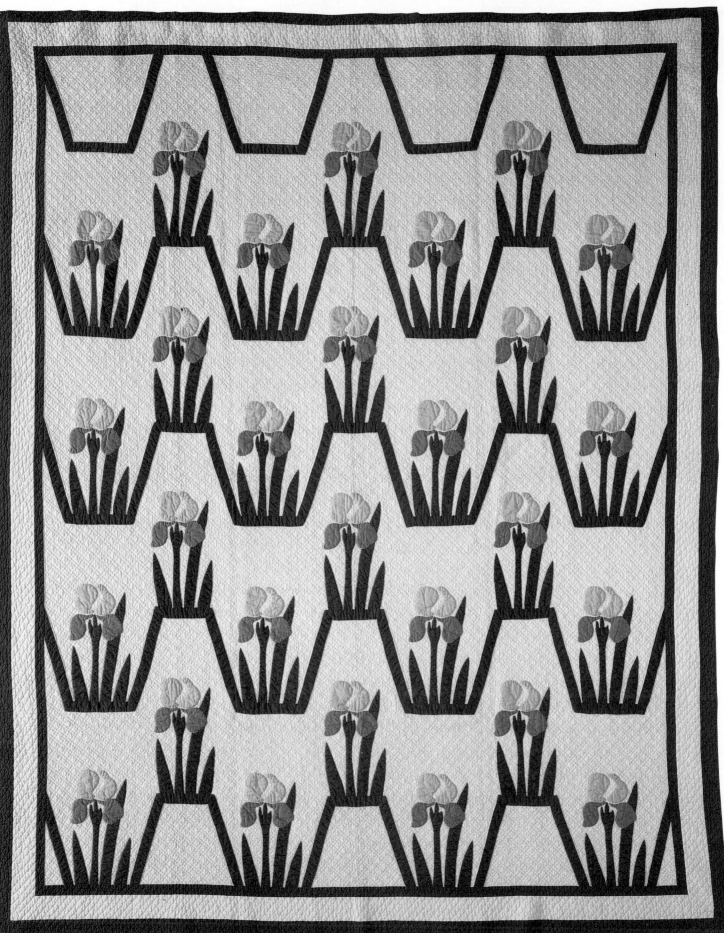

Iris

Iris is the design of Margaret Hayes, a free-lance artist who created original designs for Mountain Mist from 1928 to 1930. The coffin-shaped block is framed by garden rows that follow the block outlines. The original pattern describes a scrap quilt with blooms of many colors.

Quilt: 69½" x 84"   **Blocks: 28 (10¾" wide x 16½" high) blocks**

Iris Block—Make 28.

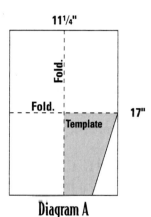

Diagram A

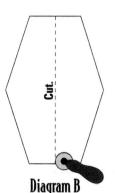

Diagram B

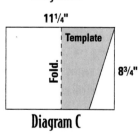

Diagram C

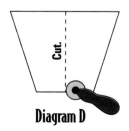

Diagram D

Materials

5¼ yards white or muslin
3½ yards green
⅜ yard purple
⅜ yard light purple
2⅛ yards 90"-wide backing fabric
72" x 90" precut batting

Cutting

Make templates for patterns A–H on page 19 and Pattern X on page 20. Add seam allowances to appliqué pieces when cutting. Cut pieces in order listed to make best use of yardage. *Note:* Side blocks and corner pieces are cut slightly oversized. These will be trimmed later after quilt is assembled.

From green, cut:
- 32" square for binding.
- 4 (2" x 88") lengthwise strips for outer border.
- 4 (1½" x 88") lengthwise strips for inner border.
- 40 (1½" x 10") strips and 28 (1½" x 7") strips for appliquéd zigzag border.
- 28 of Pattern A.
- 28 of Pattern B.
- 28 of Pattern C.
- 28 of Pattern D.

From white, cut:
- 32 (11¼" x 17") pieces. Fold each piece in quarters (Diagram A). Align X template with folds. Cut bottom and side to get 6-sided shape as shown. (Crease folds for appliqué placement lines.) Set aside 28 X pieces for blocks. Cut 4 pieces in half lengthwise (Diagram B) for side blocks.
- 8 (8" x 11¼") pieces. Fold each piece in half (Diagram C). Align X template with fold as shown and cut on bottom and side. Set aside 7 half-blocks. Cut remaining half-block in half lengthwise (Diagram D) for corner pieces.
- 8 (3"-wide) cross-grain strips for middle border.

From purple, cut:
- 28 *each* of patterns E and F.

From light purple, cut:
- 28 *each* of patterns G and H.

continued

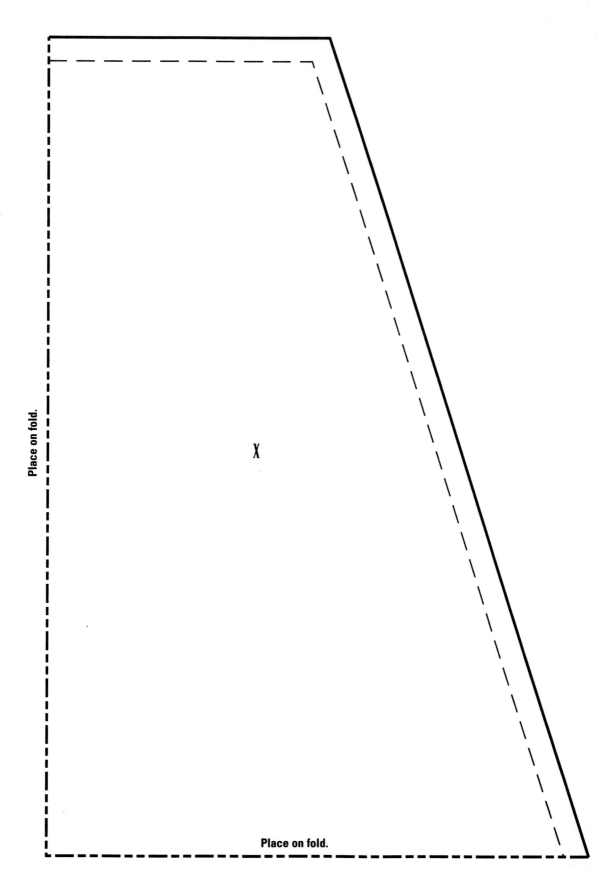

Place on fold.

X

Place on fold.

Windblown Tulip

This quilt was made in 1983 by Kathy Patrick of Nicholasville, Kentucky, from a pattern that first appeared on Mountain Mist wrappers in 1930. With its graceful border of tulips bent in the breeze, this quilt will bloom in the flower colors of your choice.

Quilt: 70½" x 87"   **Blocks: 12 (16½") squares**

Materials

4½ yards white
2¾ yards green print
1 yard green
1 yard red print
¾ yard yellow print
5¼ yards backing fabric
1 yard binding fabric
72" x 90" precut batting
17" square tracing paper
¼"-wide bias pressing bar

Cutting

Make templates for patterns A–H on pages 24 and 25. Add seam allowances to appliqué pieces when cutting. Cut pieces in order listed to make best use of yardage.

From white, cut:
- 12 (17") squares.
- 8 (6"-wide) cross-grain strips for appliquéd border.

Note: Leftover fabric will make straight-grain binding, if desired.

From green print, cut:
- 4 (3" x 91") lengthwise strips for outer borders.
- 96 of Pattern E.
- 14 of Pattern G.
- 14 of Pattern G reversed.
- 8 of Pattern H. Be sure to cut pieces for corner tulips longer as indicated on pattern.

From green, cut:
- 28" square for bias stems.
- 56 (1" x 2¾") straight-grain strips for stem A.
- 12 of Pattern B.

From red print, cut:
- 8 (1¾"-wide) cross-grain strips for middle border.
- 132 of Pattern C.

Windblown Tulip Block–Make 12.

From yellow print, cut:
- 8 (1¾"-wide) cross-grain strips for first border.
- 96 of Pattern C.

Making a Pattern

Appliqué is easier if you work with a complete tracing of the design. When appliqué is complete, save the pattern to use later to make a quilting stencil.

1. Fold paper square in half horizontally, vertically, and diagonally **(Diagram A)**, making creases for placement guides.

2. Center paper over pattern (pieces A, B, C) on page 24, aligning folds with flower stems. Trace.

3. Align drawing with C/D/E pattern on page 24, matching bottom C with tulips already drawn. Draw 8 C/D/E tulips and leaves to complete block pattern.

4. Use complete pattern to position pieces on each block using

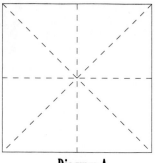

Diagram A

one of the following methods:
a) center fabric square on pattern and use a nonpermanent marker to *lightly* trace design on fabric;
b) tape pattern to a window pane; then tape fabric over it and pin appliqué pieces in place;
c) center pattern over fabric and slide appliqués into position under it, pinning pieces in place.

Preparing Stems

1. See page 160 for instructions on making continuous bias. From 28" green square, make 16¾ yards of 1"-wide bias.

2. Follow Bias Appliqué instructions on page 73 to fold, stitch, and press bias strip.

3. Cut 96 (3"-long) bias pieces for D stems and 28 (8½"-long) pieces for F stems.

4. Use same technique to fold, stitch, and press A stems.

Row Assembly Diagram

Making Blocks

See Quilt Smart Workshop, page 157, for tips on appliqué.

1. Fold and crease a white square to make placement guides **(Diagram A)**.

2. Referring to Making a Pattern, Step 4, use chosen method to position appliqués on block.

3. Starting at block center, align 4 A stems with placement lines so they cross each other at center. Appliqué stems in place. Overlap will be covered by a B circle, so clip stems in center to reduce bulk if desired.

4. Appliqué B over stem centers.

5. Pin 8 yellow C tulips in place at stem ends. Then pin D stems, E leaves, and red Cs in place.

6. Pinning tulips out of the way, appliqué Ds and Es. Then appliqué tulips to complete block.

7. Make a total of 12 blocks.

Quilt Assembly

Refer to photo and **Row Assembly Diagram** *throughout.*

1. Lay out blocks in 4 horizontal rows, with 3 blocks in each row.

2. Join blocks in each row.

3. Join rows as shown in photo.

Borders

1. Join 2 yellow print strips end-to-end to make a border for each quilt side.

2. Measure length of quilt; then trim 2 borders to match length. Sew borders to quilt sides. Press seam allowances toward borders.

3. Measure width of quilt and trim remaining borders to match quilt width. Sew borders to top and bottom edges of quilt.

4. Using red strips, repeat steps 1–3 to add next border.

5. Join 2 white strips end-to-end to make a border for each side. Referring to page 158, sew white borders to quilt and miter corners.

Appliquéd Border

Refer to photo throughout to position appliqué pieces.

1. Align an A stem with center seam of each border. Pin a shorter H leaf at bottom and a red C tulip at top of each stem. Adjust pieces as necessary to place top edge of Cs ½" below red border seam and bottom of H even with edge of white fabric. Appliqué stems; then appliqué H and C on each border.

2. Using longer H pieces, place an A/C/H tulip on each corner seam in same manner. Appliqué.

3. On each side border, pin 4 G leaves and 4 Gs reversed. Space leaves evenly between center tulip and corner of red border. Pin Fs and Cs in place. When satisfied with position of pieces, appliqué.

4. In same manner, position 3 G leaves and 3 Gs reversed on top border as shown. Pin Fs and Cs in place and appliqué. Repeat for bottom border.

5. Sew green print borders to quilt and miter corners.

continued

Bunnies

Thoughts of a baby prompted the maker to put fine hand quilting
into this little 1930s quilt. Quilted feathers frame a pair of
kissing bunnies, and more feathers undulate around the border.
Even with less quilting, such a sweet quilt is an enduring treasure.

Quilt: 45" x 54"

Materials

3 yards blue
1¾ yards white
3 yards backing fabric
72" x 90" precut batting
Black and pink embroidery floss
Tracing paper and pencil

Cutting

Make templates for patterns A and B on page 28. Add seam allowances to appliqué pieces when cutting. Cut pieces in order listed to make best use of yardage.

From blue, cut:
• 27½" x 36½" piece for center.
• 27½" square for binding.
• 2 (7½" x 57") and 2 (7½" x 48") lengthwise strips for middle border.

From white, cut:
• 4 (1½" x 57") and 4 (1½" x 48") lengthwise strips for borders.
• 1 of Pattern A.
• 1 of Pattern A reversed.
• 12 of Pattern B.

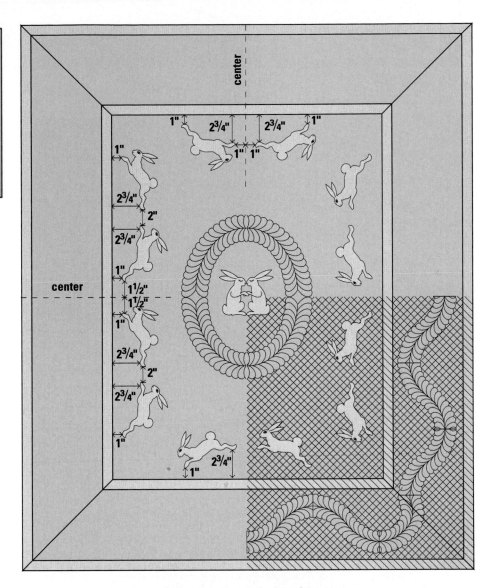

Quilt Assembly and Quilting Diagram

Quilt Assembly

1. Sew white strips to both sides of each blue border. Make 2 (57"-long) side borders and 2 (48"-long) end borders. Press seam allowances toward blue.
2. See page 158 for tips on sewing a mitered border. Sew border strips to center section and miter corners (**Quilt Assembly and Quilting Diagram**).

Appliqué

See Quilt Smart Workshop, page 157, for tips on appliqué.
1. Place each bunny appliqué piece over pattern and lightly trace embroidery lines.
2. On B bunnies, use 2 strands of pink floss to work eyes in satin stitch (stitch diagram, page 29). Use black floss to work all remaining embroidery in outline stitch (stitch diagram, page 29).
3. Turn edges of appliqué pieces as desired.

4. Fold and crease quilt top horizontally and vertically to make placement guides.
5. Center fabric over Pattern A. (If you can't see through fabric, tape a tracing to a windowpane.) Match center and placement lines of quilt with center dot and broken lines on pattern. Pin A bunnies in place, overlapping paws.
6. Referring to **Quilt Assembly Diagram**, pin 12 B bunnies in place.
7. When satisfied with placement, appliqué bunnies.

continued

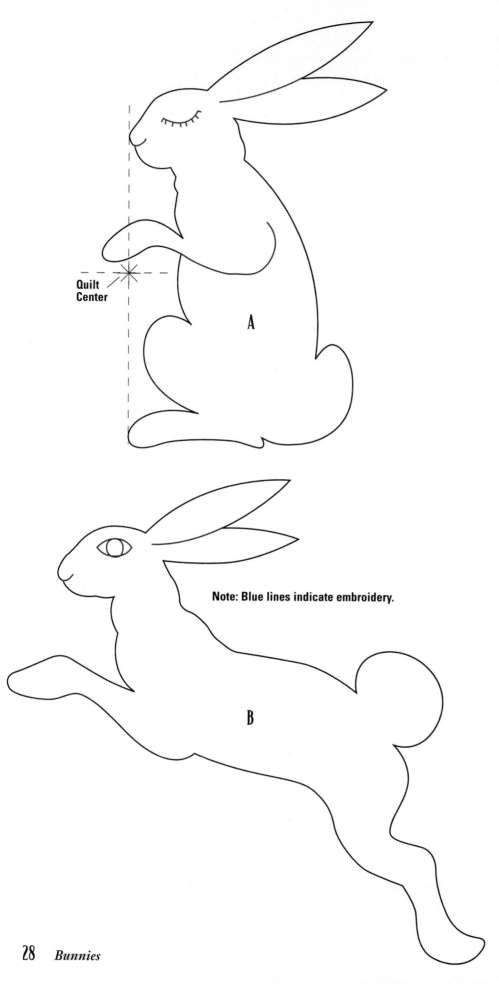

Quilt
Center

A

Note: Blue lines indicate embroidery.

B

Quilting and Finishing

Follow **Quilt Assembly and Quilting Diagram** and steps 1–6 to mark quilt with designs shown. Or choose another quilting design, if you prefer.

1. Trace Center Quilting Pattern on page 29. Darken drawing on both sides of tracing paper so you can reverse patterns as needed.

2. Tape tracing of center pattern to a light box or a bright windowpane. Lay quilt top on pattern, aligning solid lines on pattern with placement lines on quilt. (These lines are for placement only and are not to be quilted.) Lightly trace design onto fabric. Turn quilt upside down to align pattern with opposite section of oval and trace. Turn pattern over and repeat to trace design onto remaining sections of oval.

3. Make 2 tracings of Border Quilting Pattern on page 30, 1 as printed and 1 reversed. Tape drawings together, matching solid lines.

4. Center a border of quilt top over drawing with arch of pattern toward outside edge of quilt. Trace. Repeat on other borders, centering arch at bottom edge of each border. Move quilt over pattern, tracing more feathers outward from each centered arch. Red lines on diagram show pattern repeat.

5. Trace Border Corner Pattern on page 30. Place quilt top over drawing, aligning ends with feathers already drawn on borders. *Note:* On quilt shown, quilting design was probably drawn by hand, leaving no 2 corners alike. Pattern given produces a more symmetrical design.

6. Starting at center of quilt, use a ruler to lightly mark diagonal cross-hatching over remaining surface of quilt top, spacing lines ½" apart.

7. Assemble backing. Layer backing, batting, and quilt top. Baste.

8. Outline-quilt appliqués. Add more quilting as marked or as desired.

9. Make 5¾ yards of continuous bias binding. Bind quilt edges.

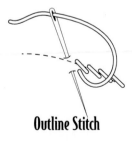

Satin Stitch

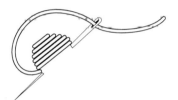

Outline Stitch

¼ Center Quilting Pattern

Border Corner Quilting Pattern

Border Quilting Pattern

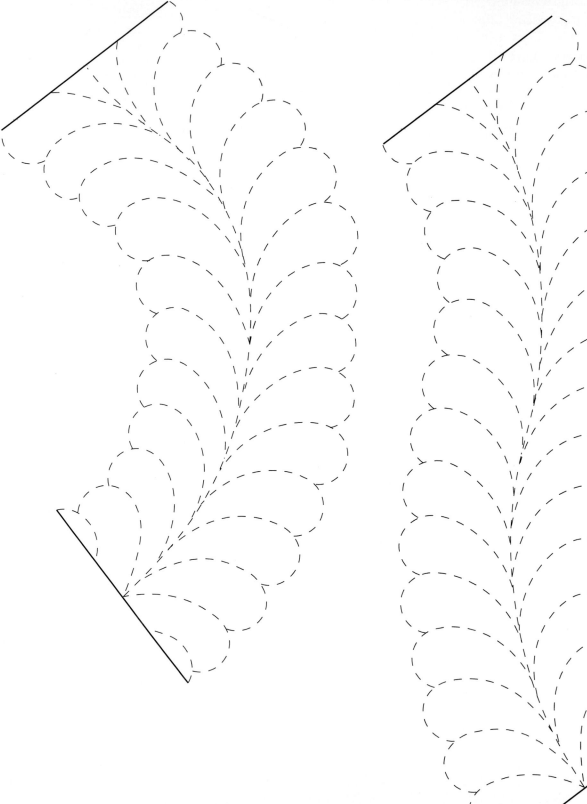

Sweet Peas

Take your pick of two versions of this quilt—a study in luscious
lavender (page 33) or a cheerful abundance of scraps (below). Added
to the Mountain Mist patterns in 1933, the design features blocks
set on point in a diagonal set and framed with a graceful border.

Quilt: 71½" x 86"   Blocks: 20 (10") squares

Materials

5⅜ yards white
1½ yards dark green*
1⅛ yards green*
1⅛ yards dark purple or
   equivalent scraps
⅞ yard lavender or equivalent
   scraps
2¼ yards 90"-wide backing fabric
81" x 96" precut batting
¼"-wide bias pressing bar
Green embroidery floss or
   quilting thread
10" square tracing paper (optional)
*Note: Scrap quilt uses 2½ yards
of 1 green fabric.

Cutting

Make templates for patterns A, C, D, and E on page 33. Add seam allowances to appliqué pieces when cutting. Cut pieces in order listed to make best use of yardage.

From white, cut:
- 2 (8" x 90") lengthwise strips and 2 (8" x 75") lengthwise strips for borders.
- 32 (10½") squares.
- 4 (15½") squares. Cut squares in quarters diagonally to get 14 setting triangles (and 2 extra).
- 2 (8") squares. Cut each square in half diagonally to get 4 corner triangles.

From dark green, cut:
- 32" square for binding.
- 80 of Pattern C for blocks.
- 92 of Pattern C reversed for border.
- 80 of Pattern A for blocks.
- 22 of Pattern A and 22 Pattern A reversed for border.

From green, cut:
- 22" square for border vine.
- 5 (2½" x 42") strips for B stems.

From dark purple or scraps, cut:
- 80 of Pattern D for blocks.
- 22 of Pattern D and 22 Pattern D reversed for border.

From lavender or scraps, cut:
- 80 of Pattern E for blocks.
- 22 of Pattern E and 22 Pattern E reversed for border.

Making Blocks

See Quilt Smart Workshop, page 157, for tips on appliqué.

1. Use 2½"-wide green strips for B stems. Measure and rotary-cut a 2½" triangle off an end of strip to establish a 45° angle for bias cuts **(Diagram A)**. Measuring from *cut* edge, rotary-cut 1"-wide strips. Each strip will be approximately 3½" long. Cut 124 B stems, 80 for blocks and 44 for border.

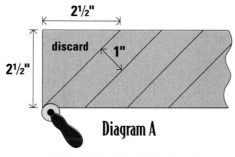

Diagram A

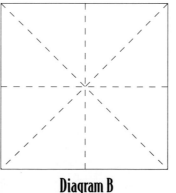

Diagram B

Sweet Peas Block—Make 20.

2. Follow Bias Appliqué instructions on page 73 to fold, stitch, and press each bias strip on pressing bar. Do not turn stem ends under, as these are covered by other pieces.

3. Fold and crease a white square to make placement guides **(Diagram B)**.

4. Pattern on page 33 is ¼ of block. Trace pattern in 4 corners of paper square to make a complete pattern.

5. Use pattern to position pieces in alphabetical order on block using one of these methods:
a) align each corner of fabric square with corner of pattern and use a nonpermanent marker to *lightly* trace design on fabric;
b) tape pattern to a windowpane; then tape fabric over pattern and pin appliqué pieces in place;
c) position tracing on fabric and slide appliqués into position under it, pinning each piece in place.

6. When satisfied with placement, appliqué pieces in alphabetical order. Pin overlapping pieces out of the way to stitch down stem.

7. Make 20 blocks.

continued

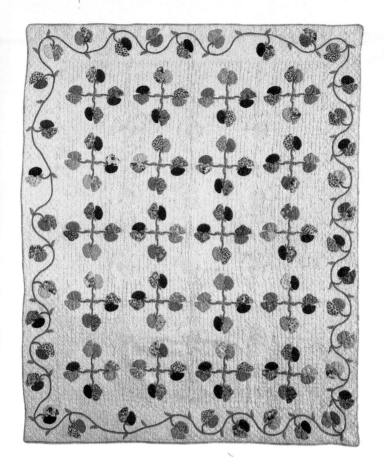

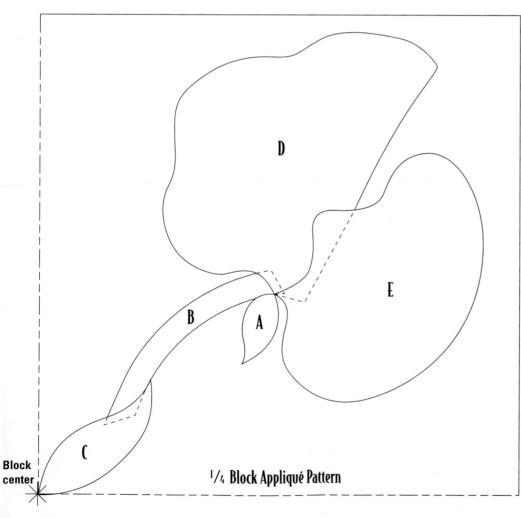

D

E

B

A

C

Block center

¹/₄ **Block Appliqué Pattern**

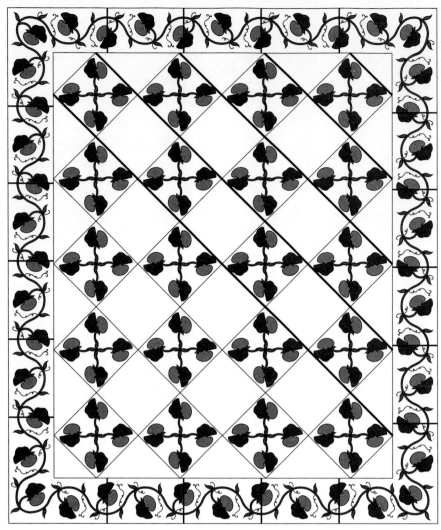

Quilt Assembly Diagram

Quilt Assembly

Refer to photos and Quilt Assembly Diagram throughout.

1. Lay out blocks in diagonal rows, indicated by red lines on diagram. Rows end with a setting triangle and/or a corner triangle.

2. When satisfied with placement, join blocks in each row.

3. Join rows as shown.

Borders

1. See page 158 for tips on sewing a mitered border. Sew border strips to quilt and miter corners.

2. Use a pin to mark center of bottom border, 1⅜" below top seam line. To mark high and low points for vine on border, measure 13"-wide segments on both sides of center, marking each spot with a pin. Then mark placement points halfway between markers, this time placing pins 1" above raw edge (red lines on Quilt Assembly Diagram indicate 13"-wide repeat of vine). Turn quilt around and repeat for top border.

3. On side borders, mark center 1" from raw edge. Measure 13" segments out from center and mark; then mark halfway points 1⅜" from seam.

4. See page 160 for instructions on making continuous bias. From 22" green square, make 12 yards of 1"-wide bias. Follow Bias Appliqué instructions on page 73 to fold, stitch, and press bias strip.

5. Starting at any side, baste prepared bias onto borders. Curve bias up and down, matching placement points. At each corner, curve bias over mitered seam to connect with next marked point. When satisfied with vine placement, trim excess bias and turn under ends.

6. Referring to photo and Quilt Assembly Diagram, place leaves, stems, and flowers along vine (see Border Pattern, page 35). Flowers facing border seam use pieces A, D, and E; flowers facing border edge use reversed patterns. All C leaves are Cs reversed.

7. When satisifed with position, appliqué pieces in place.

8. Use 2 strands of floss to embroider vine tendrils (see outline stitch diagram, page 29). Or you can quilt these lines later.

Quilting and Finishing

1. Mark quilting design on quilt top as desired. Feathered Wreath Quilting Pattern for setting squares is on page 35. Or you might prefer to use tracing of block to repeat Sweet Peas motif in setting squares and triangles.

2. Layer backing, batting, and quilt top. Baste.

3. Outline-quilt appliqué. Add additional quilting as marked or as desired. On purple quilt, quilting on blocks echoes ¼" to seam lines. Scrap quilt has cross-hatching lines quilted ½" apart.

4. Make 9 yards of continuous bias binding. Bind quilt edges.

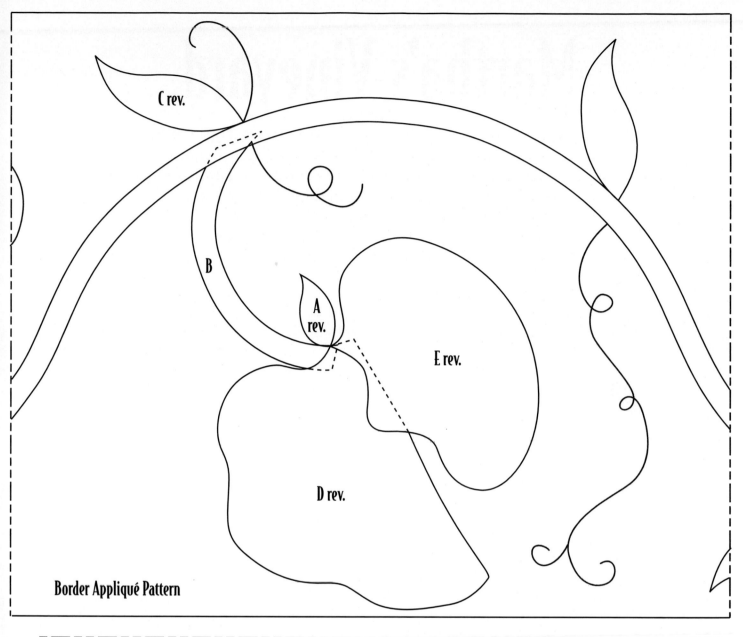

C rev.

B

A
rev.

E rev.

D rev.

Border Appliqué Pattern

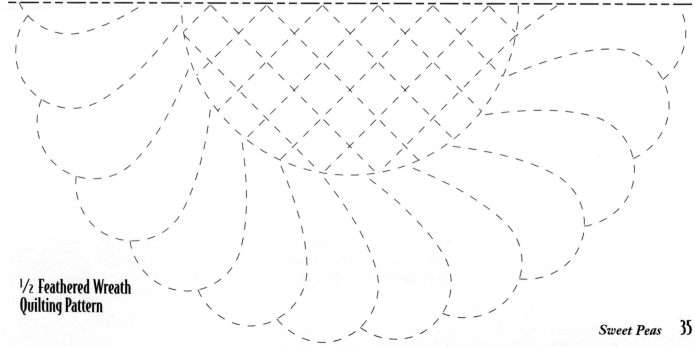

¹/₂ Feathered Wreath
Quilting Pattern

Martha's Vineyard

Challenged to interpret a Mountain Mist pattern, Darlene Scow of Salt Lake City, Utah, chose this 1931 design. Beautiful quilting in the alternate blocks helped her quilt win Best of Show in Mountain Mist's 1983 National Quilt Contest.

Quilt: 80" x 96"   Blocks: 12 (16") squares

Materials

5¾ yards white
3 yards olive
1⅛ yards green print
⅞ yard rose print
2⅞ yards 90"-wide backing fabric
90" x 108" precut batting
16" square tracing paper
¼"-wide bias pressing bar

Cutting

Make templates for patterns B, C, and D on page 38. Add seam allowances to appliqué pieces when cutting. Cut pieces in order listed to make best use of yardage.

From white, cut:
• 12 (16½") squares.
• 2 (12¾" x 100") lengthwise strips and 2 (12¾" x 84") lengthwise strips for middle border.

From green print, cut:
• 96 of Pattern B.
• 24 of Pattern C.

From rose print, cut:
• 660 of Pattern D.

From olive, cut:
• 2 (3" x 100") lengthwise strips and 2 (3" x 84") lengthwise strips for outer border.
• 2 (1½" x 100") lengthwise strips and 2 (1½" x 84") lengthwise strips for inner border.
• 34" square for binding.
• 30" square for bias vines.
• 22" square for bias stems.

Making a Pattern

Appliqué is easier if you work with a complete tracing of the design. The patterns on pages 38 and 39 represent ½ of block. Follow these directions to make a complete pattern.
1. Fold paper square in half vertically, horizontally, and diagonally, making creases for placement guides **(Diagram A)**.
2. Match 1 corner of paper with pattern on page 38. Align center guidelines with dotted lines on pattern. Trace Section 1.
3. Match adjacent corner of paper with pattern on page 39, again aligning center guidelines. Trace Section 2.
4. Turn paper around and repeat, tracing both sections again to complete pattern **(Diagram B)**.

continued

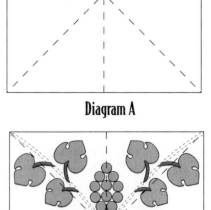

Martha's Vineyard Block–Make 6.

Diagram A

Diagram B

Preparing Stems

1. Cut 22" square of olive into 1"-wide bias strips.

2. Follow Bias Appliqué instructions on page 73 to fold, stitch, and press each bias strip.

3. Cut 188 (2"-long) pieces for A stems, 96 for blocks and 92 for appliquéd border.

Making Appliquéd Blocks

See Quilt Smart Workshop, page 157, for tips on appliqué.

1. Fold and crease a white square to make placement guides.

2. Position pieces A, B, C, and D in alphabetical order on block using one of these methods:

a) align fabric square with pattern, matching edges and placement lines; use a nonpermanent marker to *lightly* trace design on fabric; b) tape pattern to a windowpane; then tape fabric over pattern and pin appliqué pieces in place; c) center tracing on fabric and slide appliqués under it, pinning each piece in place.

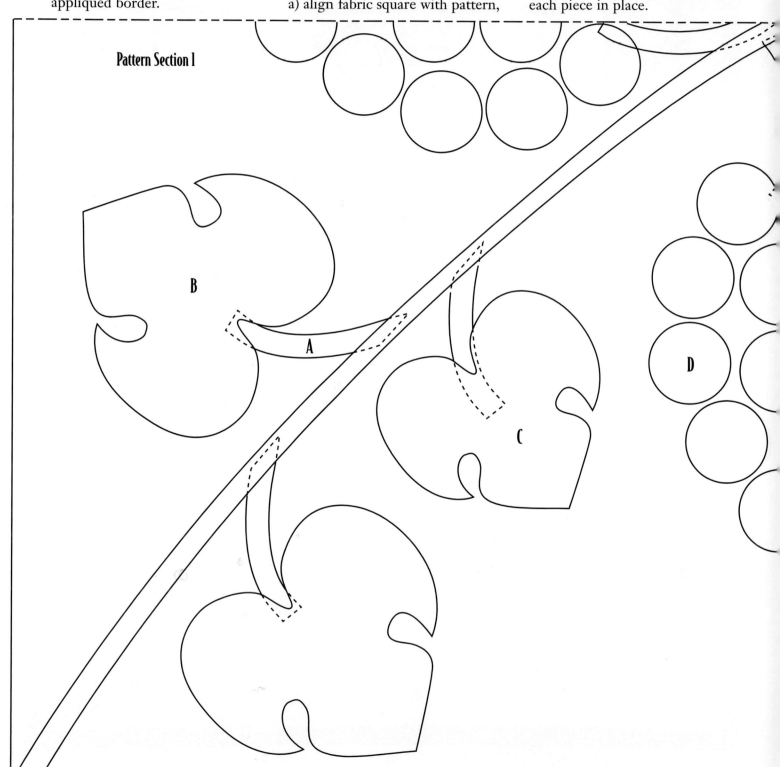

Pattern Section 1

3. When all pieces are pinned on block, *lightly* trace placement line for vine **(Diagram B).**

4. When satisfied with placement, appliqué pieces in alphabetical order. Pin overlapping pieces out of the way to sew stems. Stem ends will be covered by vine later.

5. Appliqué 6 blocks.

Marking Alternate Blocks

See Quilt Smart Workshop, page 159, for tips on marking quilting designs.

1. Fold and crease 6 white squares to make placement guides.

2. Grape Wreath Quilting Pattern on page 41 is ¼ of quilting design. Align placement lines

on fabric square center with placement lines of pattern and use a nonpermanent marker to *lightly* trace design on each square.

continued

Pattern Section 2

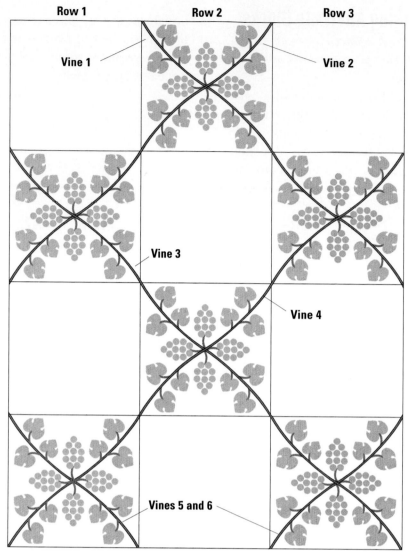

Row 1 Row 2 Row 3

Vine 1

Vine 2

Vine 3

Vine 4

Vines 5 and 6

Quilt Assembly Diagram

Quilt Assembly

Refer to photo and Quilt Assembly Diagram *throughout.*

1. For each row, select 2 appliquéd blocks and 2 alternate blocks. Lay out blocks in 3 vertical rows, alternating block types as shown. (Row 2 is same as rows 1 and 3, turned upside down.)

2. Join blocks in each row.

3. Join rows as shown.

Vine Appliqué

1. See page 160 for instructions on making continuous bias. From 30" square of olive, make 18⅝ yards of 1"-wide bias.

2. Follow Bias Appliqué instructions on page 73 to fold, stitch, and press bias strip.

3. Cut and set aside 4 (90"-long) bias pieces for border. Cut 2 (52") lengths for vines 1 and 2, 77" lengths for vines 3 and 4, and 26" lengths for vines 5 and 6.

4. Pin vines 1 and 2 in place on block at top of Row 2, aligning ends of bias with raw edges at top of block. Pin vines across seam lines and onto blocks in rows 1 and 3. Pin remaining vines on blocks in same manner.

5. When satisfied with placement, appliqué vine. Trim ends when appliqué is complete.

Borders

1. Sew narrow and wide olive strips to sides of each white border. Make 2 (100"-long) borders and 2 (84"-long) borders.

2. See page 158 for tips on sewing a mitered border. Sew border strips to quilt and miter corners.

3. Use a pin to mark center of bottom white border, 4¾" from top seam line. To mark high and low points for vine along border, measure 16"-wide segments on both sides of center, marking each spot with a pin 4¾" below top seam (Diagram C). Then mark placement points halfway between markers, this time pinning 4¾" above bottom seam. Turn quilt around and repeat for top border. Place 7 pins on each border.

4. To mark vine placement on side borders, mark center 4¾" from outer seam. Measure 16" segments out from center and mark; then mark halfway points 4¾" from inner seam as shown.

5. Starting at any side, baste prepared bias strip onto each border. Curve bias up and down, to match pin placement points and removing pins as you go. At each corner, curve bias over mitered seam to make a heart shape. When satisfied with position of bias, trim excess bias and turn under ends.

6. Place leaves, stems, and grape clusters along vine as desired (Diagram D). Use 8 grapes (D) in each cluster as shown. When satisifed with position, appliqué vines, stems, leaves, and grapes in place.

Diagram D

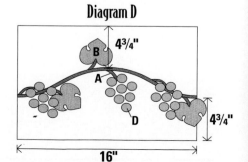

B 4¾"

A

D

4¾"

16"

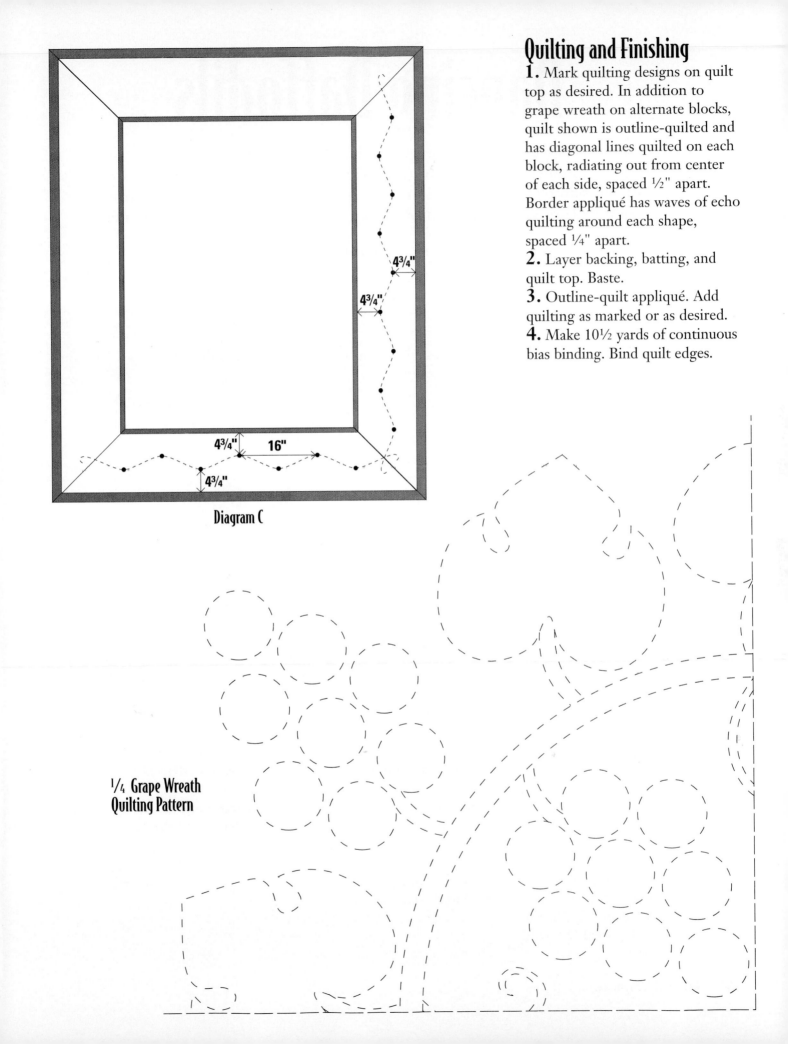

Quilting and Finishing

1. Mark quilting designs on quilt top as desired. In addition to grape wreath on alternate blocks, quilt shown is outline-quilted and has diagonal lines quilted on each block, radiating out from center of each side, spaced ½" apart. Border appliqué has waves of echo quilting around each shape, spaced ¼" apart.

2. Layer backing, batting, and quilt top. Baste.

3. Outline-quilt appliqué. Add quilting as marked or as desired.

4. Make 10½ yards of continuous bias binding. Bind quilt edges.

4¾"

4¾"

4¾"   16"

4¾"

Diagram C

¼ Grape Wreath Quilting Pattern

Dancing Daffodils

The classic poem below inspired this lovely quilt, made in 1944 by Mrs. Blaine Wilson of Sturgeon, Kentucky. The fabrics are classic Depression-era greens, brightened with yellow and cream. Let your imagination grow a garden of flowers in a field of your favorite hue.

Quilt: 72" x 88"   Blocks: 20 (16") squares

The Daffodils

I wandered lonely as a cloud
That floats on high o'er vales
*   and hills,*
When all at once I saw a crowd,
A host, of golden daffodils;
Beside the lake, beneath the trees,
Fluttering and dancing in the breeze.

Continuous as the stars that shine
And twinkle on the milky way,
They stretched in never-ending line
Along the margin of a bay;
Ten thousand saw I at a glance,
Tossing their heads in sprightly dance.

The waves beside them danced;
*   but they*
Outdid the sparkling waves in glee;
A poet could not but be gay,
In such a jocund company;
I gazed—and gazed—but little thought
What wealth the show to me had
*   brought.*

For oft, when on my couch I lie
In vacant or in pensive mood,
They flash upon that inward eye
Which is the bliss of solitude;
And then my heart with pleasure fills,
And dances with the daffodils.
        William Wordsworth
    English poet, 1770–1850

Materials

4¾ yards light green
2½ yards cream
2½ yards dark green
1⅞ yards medium green
¾ yard yellow
5¼ yards backing fabric
81" x 96" precut batting
Tracing paper and pencil
¼"-wide bias pressing bar

Cutting

Make templates for patterns A, D, E, F, and G on page 45. Add seam allowances to appliqué pieces when cutting. Cut pieces in order listed to make best use of yardage.

From light green, cut:
- 20 (16½") squares.
- 2 (2" x 86") lengthwise strips and 2 (2" x 73") lengthwise strips for middle border.

From cream, cut:
- 2 (1½" x 90") lengthwise strips and 2 (1½" x 76") lengthwise strips for outer border.
- 80 of Pattern E.
- 80 of Pattern F.

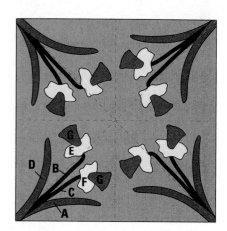

Dancing Daffodils Block—Make 20.

From dark green, cut:
- 32" square for binding.
- 6 (4¾"-wide) cross-grain strips for B and C bias stems.
- 2 (2" x 83") lengthwise strips and 2 (2" x 70") lengthwise strips for first border.

From medium green, cut:
- 80 of Pattern A.
- 80 of Pattern D.

From yellow, cut:
- 160 of Pattern G.

continued

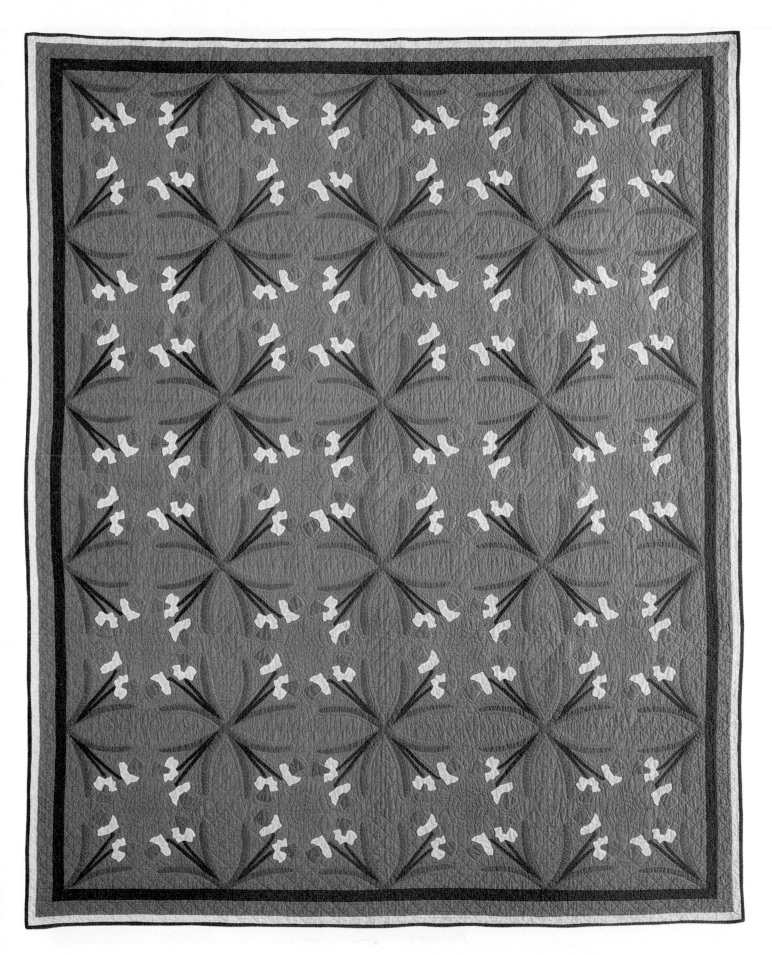

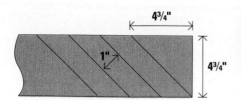

Diagram A

Row Assembly Diagram

Preparing Stems

1. Stems are cut from 4¾"-wide dark green strips. First measure and rotary-cut a 4¾" triangle off an end of strip to establish a 45° angle **(Diagram A)**. Measuring from *cut* edge, rotary-cut 1"-wide strips. Cut 160 bias strips.

2. Follow Bias Appliqué instructions on page 73 to fold, stitch, and press bias strips on ¼"-wide pressing bar. Do not turn stem ends under, as these will be covered by flowers.

3. Trim 80 strips to 6½" long for B stems. Trim remaining 80 strips to 6" long for C stems.

Making Blocks

See Quilt Smart Workshop, page 157, for tips on appliqué.

1. Fold and crease a light green square to make placement guides **(Diagram B)**.

2. Pattern on page 45 is ¼ of block. Copy pattern onto tracing paper. Align each corner of fabric square with corner of pattern and

use a nonpermanent marker to *lightly* trace design on fabric. This is a good time to mark Spider Web quilting design (shown on pattern) at center of each block.

3. Align A, B, C, and D stems with block corner, overlapping pieces as shown. (Do not turn stem ends under at corner, as these are sewn into the seam when blocks are joined.) Appliqué stems in alphabetical order, pinning overlapping pieces out of the way as you stitch bottom pieces.

4. Pin E and F pieces at ends of stems. Lay Gs over E and F as

shown on pattern. When satisfied with placement, appliqué pieces in alphabetical order. Pin Gs out of the way to stitch Es and Fs.

5. Complete appliqué in 4 corners of block in same manner.

6. Make 20 blocks.

Quilt Assembly

Refer to photo and Row Assembly Diagram *throughout.*

1. Lay out blocks in 5 horizontal rows, with 4 blocks in each row.

2. Join blocks in each row.

3. Join rows as shown in photo.

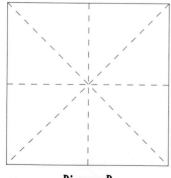

Diagram B

Quilting Diagram

Borders

1. Measure length of quilt; then trim 2 dark green borders to match quilt length. Sew borders to quilt sides.

2. Measure width of quilt; trim remaining dark green borders to match quilt width. Sew borders to top and bottom edges of quilt.

3. Repeat steps 1 and 2 to add light green border; then add cream border in same manner.

Quilting and Finishing

1. Mark quilting design on quilt top as shown or as desired.

2. Use a ruler to mark diagonal cross-hatching over flowers around outside edge of quilt and into borders, spacing lines 1" apart.

3. Assemble backing. Layer backing, batting, and quilt top. Baste.

4. Outline-quilt appliqués. Add more quilting as desired.

5. Make 9¼ yards of continuous bias binding. Bind quilt edges.

Block Center

Spider Web Quilting Pattern

G

E

D

B

C

A

F

G

¼ Block Appliqué Pattern

Chanticleer

Ten appliquéd roosters will have chicken-lovers crying *fowl!* This
Margaret Hayes design, made in 1940 by Mrs. Charles Poole, honors
the cocky character of French folklore. Sashed blocks are framed by
a border of round little chicks just out of their embroidered shells.

Quilt: 67¼" x 81"   Blocks: 10 (12") appliquéd squares
                                      10 (12") embroidered squares

Materials

3¼ yards white or muslin
3 yards red
¾ yard rose
½ yard yellow
½ yard orange
⅛ yard tan
2⅛ yards 90"-wide backing fabric
72" x 90" precut batting
Black, red, gold, and ivory
   embroidery floss
2 (12") squares tracing paper

Cutting

Make templates for appliqué patterns A–N and Pattern X on pages 50, 51, and 52. Add seam allowances to appliqué pieces when cutting. Cut pieces in order listed to make best use of yardage.

From white, cut:
- 20 (12½") squares.
- 4 (3¾" x 72") lengthwise strips for appliquéd border.

From red, cut:
- 4 (2" x 85") lengthwise strips for outer borders.
- 7 (2¼" x 72") lengthwise strips for vertical sashing and inner border.
- 32" square for binding.
- 16 (2¼" x 12½") horizontal sashing strips.
- 2 (4⅝") squares. Cut each square in half to get 4 X triangles. Or use X template to cut 4 triangles.
- 10 of Pattern A.
- 10 of Pattern D.

From orange, cut:
- 10 of Pattern L.
- 20 of Pattern B.
- 10 of Pattern E.

From rose, cut:
- 8 (1"-wide) cross-grain strips for narrow border.
- 2 (4⅝") squares. Cut each square in half to get 4 X triangles. Or use X template to cut 4 triangles.
- 10 of Pattern C.
- 10 of Pattern I.

From yellow, cut:
- 18 of Pattern M.
- 18 of Pattern N.
- 10 of Pattern K.
- 20 of Pattern H.

From tan, cut:
- 10 of Pattern F.
- 10 of Pattern G.
- 10 of Pattern J.

Making a Pattern

Appliqué is easier if you work with a tracing of the complete design.

1. Fold paper square in half horizontally and vertically, making creases for placement guides.

2. Center paper over rooster pattern on page 50 (pieces A, B, G, H, I, J, K, and L). Align fold lines with block center marked on pattern. (Bottom of foot, Pattern H, should be 1" from bottom edge of paper.) Trace. Include markings for underlap of piece F.

3. Place drawing over pattern on next page (pieces C, D, E, F, and H), aligning it with parts of A, B, and G already traced. Trace patterns to complete block pattern.

4. Use complete pattern to position appliqué pieces on each block using one of these methods:
a) center fabric square on pattern and use a nonpermanent marker to *lightly* trace design on fabric;

Rooster Block—Make 10.

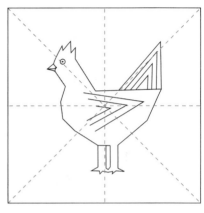

Hen Block—Make 10.

b) tape pattern to a windowpane; then tape fabric over pattern and pin appliqué pieces in place;
c) center pattern over fabric and slide appliqués under it, pinning each piece in place.

Making Rooster Blocks

See Quilt Smart Workshop, page 157, for tips on appliqué.

1. Turn under edges on 2 sides of each B triangle. Align unturned edge with edge of A as shown on pattern. Appliqué Bs onto A.

2. Machine-stitch C to A/B piece to make rooster body. Turn edges on A/B/C as 1 piece.

3. Prepare all remaining pieces for appliqué. It is not necessary to turn edges that will be covered by another piece. *continued*

Quilt Assembly

Refer to photo and Quilt Assembly Diagram *throughout.*

1. Lay out blocks in 4 vertical rows, with 5 blocks in each row, placing sashing strips between blocks. Alternate Rooster and Hen blocks in each row as shown. Make 2 of Row 1, starting with a Hen block, and 2 of Row 2, starting with a Rooster block.

2. Join blocks and sashing strips in each row.

3. Measure length of each row. If measurements are not the same, average the measurements. (Add the lengths of longest and shortest and divide by 2.) Trim 3 vertical sashing strips to fit.

4. Join rows and sashing strips as shown, easing to fit as necessary.

Borders

1. See page 158 for tips on sewing a mitered corner. Sew 2¼" red borders to quilt and miter corners.

2. Measure length and width of quilt through middle of quilt. Trim white borders to match quilt length and width, but do not sew them onto quilt yet.

3. Trace detail lines onto chick appliqués (M and N).

4. Fold each white border strip in half to find center. Place center between Eggshell Embroidery patterns on page 52. Lightly trace patterns onto fabric. (Eggshells will be ¾" apart.) Referring to photo, pin pairs of chicks in place and trace additional eggshells as shown. Last eggshell will be ¾" from end of each border strip.

5. When satisfied with position, appliqué chicks in place.

6. Use 2 strands of gold floss to work chick details in outline stitch. Make white French knots

4. Trace eye outlines onto Ls.

5. Fold and crease white square to make placement guides.

6. Referring to Making a Pattern, Step 4, use chosen method to position appliqués. Where G and A meet, butt pieces together or clip seam allowance of A to let it underlap G.

7. When satisfied with position of each piece, appliqué pieces in alphabetical order. Pin overlapping pieces out of the way to stitch underlying pieces.

8. Appliqué 10 blocks.

9. Use 2 strands of red floss to work an outline stitch for outer eye and ivory floss to work satin stitch for inner eye. (See stitch diagrams, page 29.)

Making Hen Blocks

1. Fold paper square in half horizontally and vertically, making creases for placement guides.

2. Center paper over hen pattern on page 53. Align fold lines with center marked on pattern. (Head and feet should be 2" from edges of paper.) Trace.

3. Center fabric square on pattern. Use a nonpermanent marker to *lightly* trace design on fabric.

4. Use 2 strands of red floss to work hen in outline stitch. Make a French knot for hen's inner eye.

5. Embroider 10 hen blocks.

for chicks' inner eyes. Use 2 strands of black floss to work eggshells in outline stitch.

7. Join 2 rose strips end-to-end to make a border for each side. Sew a rose border to each white border; trim excess fabric.

8. Sew shorter borders to top and bottom edges of quilt. Press seam allowances toward red.

9. Join red and rose X triangles to make 4 corner squares. Sew a square to both ends of each side border strip, positioning rose triangle against border. Press seam allowances toward triangles.

10. Sew side borders to quilt, matching corner seam with top and bottom border seams and easing to fit as needed.

11. Sew remaining red borders to quilt and miter corners.

Quilting and Finishing

1. Mark quilting design on quilt top as desired. **Quilting Diagram** shows 2 blocks and part of border quilted as shown. Appliqué and embroidery motifs are outline-quilted. Diagonal lines fill background of each block, spaced ½" apart. Hen body is quilted in a clamshell pattern to simulate feathers.

2. Trace Rope Quilting Pattern on page 53. Cut out tracing, leaving 1" of paper around drawing. Put a large needle in your sewing machine and machine-stitch on lines of drawing to make a stencil. Center stencil at 1 end of each sashing strip and mark; then reposition pattern to mark second half of sashing strip. Mark a square at each sashing corner as shown.

3. Layer backing, batting, and quilt top. Baste.

4. Quilt as marked or as desired.

5. Make 8¾ yards of continuous bias binding. Bind quilt edges.

Quilt Assembly Diagram

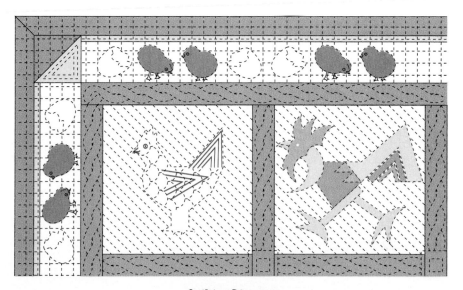

Quilting Diagram

Chanticleer **49**

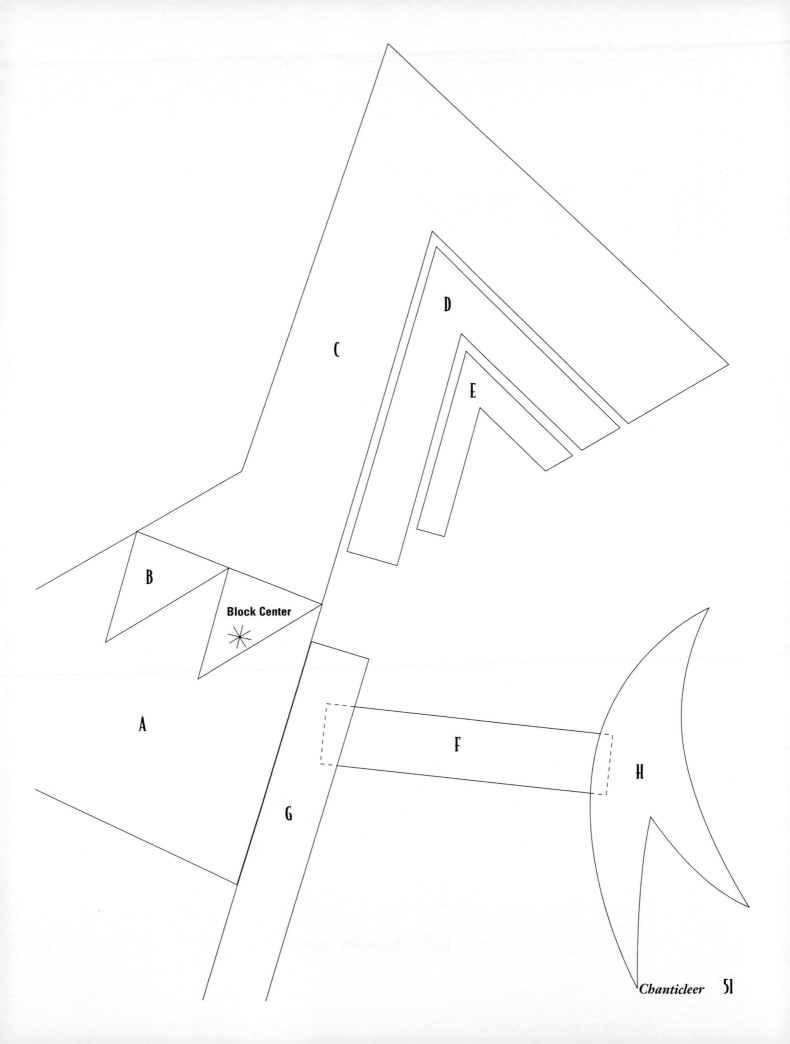

A

B

C

D

E

Block Center

F

G

H

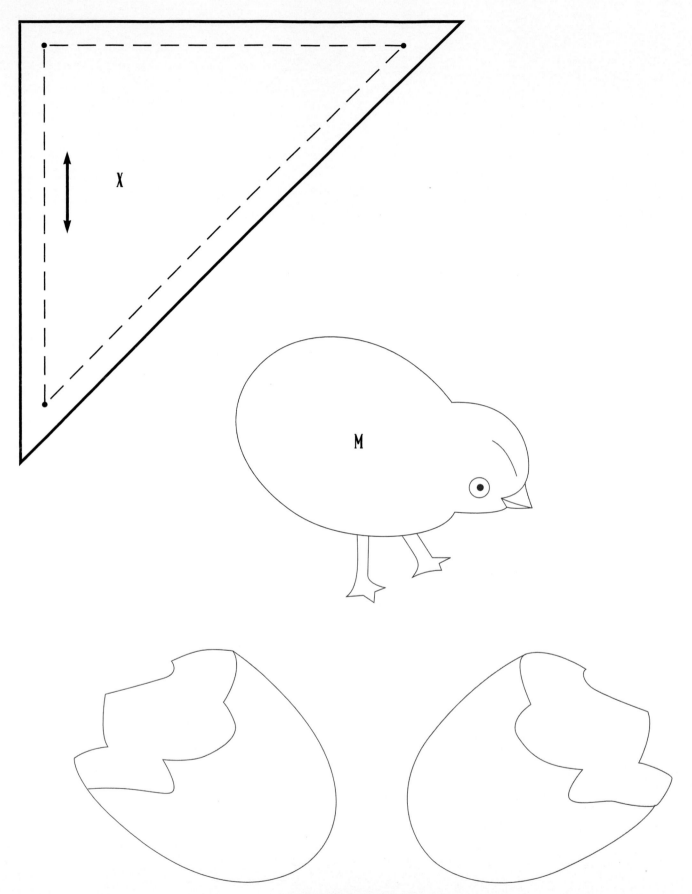

X

M

Eggshells Embroidery Pattern

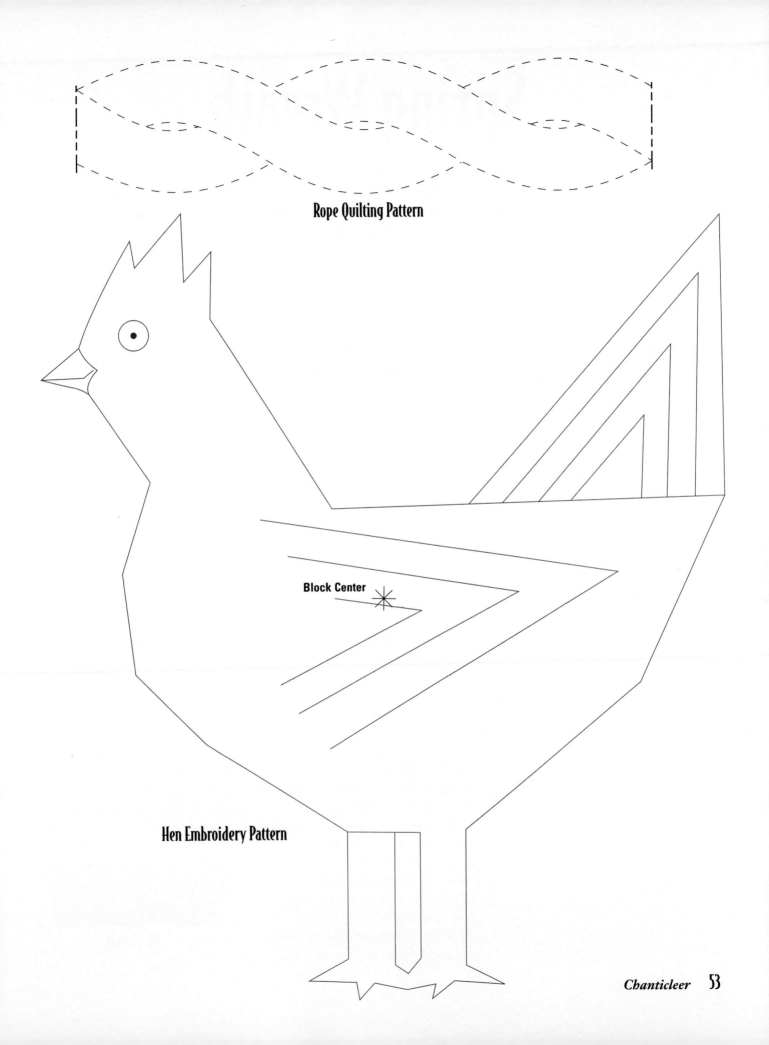

Rope Quilting Pattern

Block Center

Hen Embroidery Pattern

Spring Wreath

Flowers have inspired many a quilter to appliqué a garden of fabric blossoms. This classic rose wreath design became a Mountain Mist pattern in 1945. Our crisp blue and white interpretation was made by Mrs. H. A. Coulter of Barnville, Ohio, in 1949.

Quilt: 74" x 94"   **Blocks: 18 (14") squares**

Materials

5 yards blue
3¾ yards white
5¾ yards backing fabric
81" x 96" precut batting
¼"-wide bias pressing bar
14" square tracing paper

Cutting

Make templates for patterns A, C, D, and E on page 57. Add seam allowances to appliqué pieces when cutting. Cut pieces in order listed to make best use of yardage.

From blue, cut:
- 4 (8" x 84") lengthwise strips for borders.
- 36" square for binding.
- 6 (3¼"-wide) cross-grain strips for B bias stems.
- 576 of Pattern A.
- 72 of Pattern C.
- 72 of Pattern D.
- 72 of Pattern E.

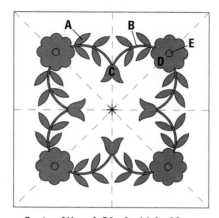

Spring Wreath Block–Make 18.

From white, cut:
- 18 (14½") squares.
- 3 (21") squares. Cut each square in quarters diagonally to get 10 setting triangles (and 2 extra).
- 2 (10¾") squares. Cut each square in half diagonally to get 4 corner triangles.

Making Blocks

See Quilt Smart Workshop, page 157, for tips on appliqué.

1. Fold and crease paper to make placement guides (Diagram A).
2. Pattern on page 57 is ¼ of block. Trace pattern in 4 corners of paper square to make a complete pattern.
3. Fold and crease a white fabric square to make placement guides.

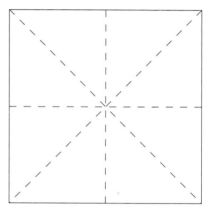

Diagram A

4. Cut B stems from 3¼"-wide blue strips. Measure and rotary-cut a 3¼" triangle off an end of strip to establish a 45° angle for bias cuts (Diagram B). Measuring from *cut* edge, rotary-cut 1"-wide strips. Each strip is about 4½" long. Cut 144 B stems.
5. Follow Bias Appliqué instructions on page 73 to fold, stitch, and press bias strips on ¼"-wide pressing bar. Do not turn stem ends under, as these will be covered by flowers. *continued*

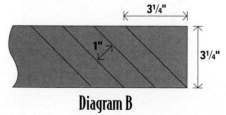

Diagram B

Row 1   Row 2   Row 3

Quilt Assembly Diagram

6. Use pattern to position pieces in alphabetical order on fabric using one of these methods: a) align each corner of fabric square with corner of pattern; use a nonpermanent marker to *lightly* trace design directly onto fabric; b) tape traced pattern to a windowpane; then tape fabric over pattern and pin pieces in place; c) position tracing on fabric and slide appliqués under it, pinning each piece in place.
7. When satisfied with placement, appliqué leaves, stems, and flowers in alphabetical order. Pin stems out of the way to stitch down A leaves.
8. Add E flower centers to complete appliqué.
9. Make 18 blocks.

Quilt Assembly

Refer to photo and Quilt Assembly Diagram *throughout.*

1. Lay out blocks in 6 diagonal rows. For Row 1, lay out a corner triangle, 5 blocks, and a setting triangle. For Row 2, lay out 3 blocks with a setting triangle at

Signature Patch

When you sign and date a quilt, you send a little of yourself into the future. Most antique quilts are anonymous, like empty pages where there should be history about people and family. Future generations will appreciate having a record of who made each quilt and why.

There are several ways to permanently mark a quilt, on the front or back. The most popular is a signature patch,

sometimes called a memory patch, sewn onto the backing.

This label can include your name, town, date on which the quilt was completed, who it was made for, and any special occasion connected with the quilt.

A practical label is a piece of muslin, hemmed on all sides. To stabilize the fabric for writing, press freezer paper to the back, coated side against the muslin. Use a fine-tip permanent pen to write your message; then peel off the paper and handstitch the label to the quilt back.

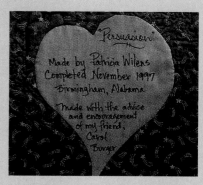

You can use embroidery and cross-stitch to make lovely signature patches. Incorporating a name and date in the quilting design is another excellent way to personalize your quilt.

both ends of row. Select 1 block for Row 3 and add setting triangles to opposite sides and a corner triangle on a third side. Working out from center, lay out 2 of each row as shown.

2. When satisfied with placement, join blocks in each row.

3. Join rows as shown.

Border

1. Measure length of quilt. Trim 2 borders to match quilt length. Sew borders to quilt sides. Press seam allowances toward borders.

2. Measure width of quilt and trim remaining borders to match quilt width. Sew borders to top and bottom edges of quilt.

Quilting and Finishing

1. Mark quilting design on quilt top as desired. Block design is on pattern below. Cross-hatching, spaced ¾" apart, is quilted in borders.

2. Assemble backing. Layer backing, batting, and quilt top. Baste.

3. Quilt as desired.

4. Make 9⅝ yards of continuous bias binding. Bind quilt edges.

¼ Block Appliqué Pattern

Block center

A

B

C

D

E

Iris Bed

The stems and leaves of these colorful irises are appliquéd over the seam lines of the assembled quilt top, blurring the blocks into an allover design. Appliquéd blocks and half-blocks are balanced by plain squares, beautifully quilted in a feathered wreath pattern.

Quilt: 76" x 90"   **Blocks: 7 (15") squares**
Half-Blocks: 10 (7½" x 15")

Materials

5⅜ yards light green
3¾ yards green
1 yard *each* light blue and pink
⅜ yard *each* blue and dark pink
¼ yard yellow
⅛ yard or scraps orange
5½ yards backing fabric
81" x 96" precut batting
15" square tracing paper
½"-wide bias pressing bar

Cutting

Make templates for patterns A, B, C, E, F, and G on page 61. Add seam allowances to appliqué pieces when cutting. Cut pieces in order listed to make best use of yardage.

From light green, cut:
- 15 (15½") squares.
- 4 (8") corner squares.
- 16 (8" x 15½") half-block pieces.
- 2 (8½" x 92") lengthwise strips for border.

From light blue, cut:
- 24 of Pattern A.
- 24 of Pattern A reversed.
- 24 of Pattern C.
- 24 of Pattern C reversed.

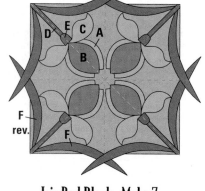

Iris Bed Block—Make 7.

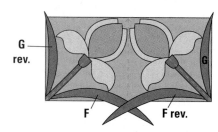

Iris Bed Half-Block—Make 10.

From blue, cut:
- 24 of Pattern B.

From pink, cut:
- 20 of Pattern A.
- 20 of Pattern A reversed.
- 20 of Pattern C.
- 20 of Pattern C reversed.

From dark pink, cut:
- 20 of Pattern B.

From yellow, cut:
- 4 of Pattern A.
- 4 of Pattern A reversed.
- 4 of Pattern C.
- 4 of Pattern C reversed.

From orange, cut:
- 4 of Pattern B.

From green, cut:
- 34" square for binding.
- 24 (1½" x 9") strips for D stems.
- 38 of Pattern F.
- 38 of Pattern F reversed.
- 10 of Pattern G.
- 10 of Pattern G reversed.
- 48 of Pattern E.

Making a Pattern

Appliqué is easier if you work with a complete tracing of the design. Pattern on page 61 is ¼ of block. Follow these directions to make a complete pattern.

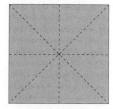

Diagram A

1. Fold paper square in half vertically, horizontally, and diagonally, making creases for placement guides **(Diagram A)**.

continued

continued

2. Match a corner of paper with corner of pattern on page 61, aligning guidelines with lines on pattern. Trace. (Partial outline of leaves is sufficient, as these are appliquéd after blocks are joined.)

3. Reposition paper to trace next corner, aligning guidelines. Trace all 4 corners to complete pattern.

Making Appliquéd Blocks

See Quilt Smart Workshop, page 157, for tips on appliqué.

1. Fold and crease all light green squares to make placement guides.

2. Align fabric square with traced pattern, matching edges and placement lines. Center flowers and stems on diagonal lines. Use a nonpermanent marker to *lightly* trace design on fabric. Pin A, B, and C pieces on block.

3. Flowers should be 2" apart, centered on guidelines. When satisfied with placement, appliqué pieces in alphabetical order. Pin overlapping pieces out of the way to stitch first pieces. Bottom of flower will be covered by E later.

4. Appliqué 6 blue blocks and 1 yellow/orange block.

5. In same manner, trace pattern onto 2 corners of 10 half-blocks. Appliqué 10 pink half-blocks.

Marking Alternate Blocks

See Quilt Smart Workshop, page 159, for tips on marking quilting designs.

1. Feathered Wreath Quilting Pattern on page 62 is ½ of block design. Align placement lines on fabric square with center line of pattern and use a nonpermanent marker to *lightly* trace design on each alternate square.

2. Mark pattern on 6 half-blocks and 4 corner squares.

Quilt Assembly

Refer to **Row Assembly Diagram** *throughout.*

1. For Row 1, lay out 2 appliquéd half-blocks, 1 plain half-block, and 2 corner squares in a row, alternating blocks as shown. Lay out 2 of Row 1.

2. For Row 2, select 1 appliquéd block, 2 plain blocks, and 2 appliquéd half-blocks. Lay out 2 rows with blue

continued

Row 1—Make 2.

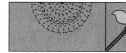

Row 2—Make 3.

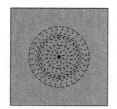
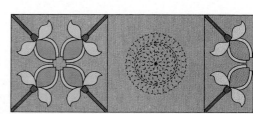

Row 3—Make 2.

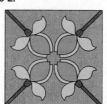

Row Assembly Diagram

F

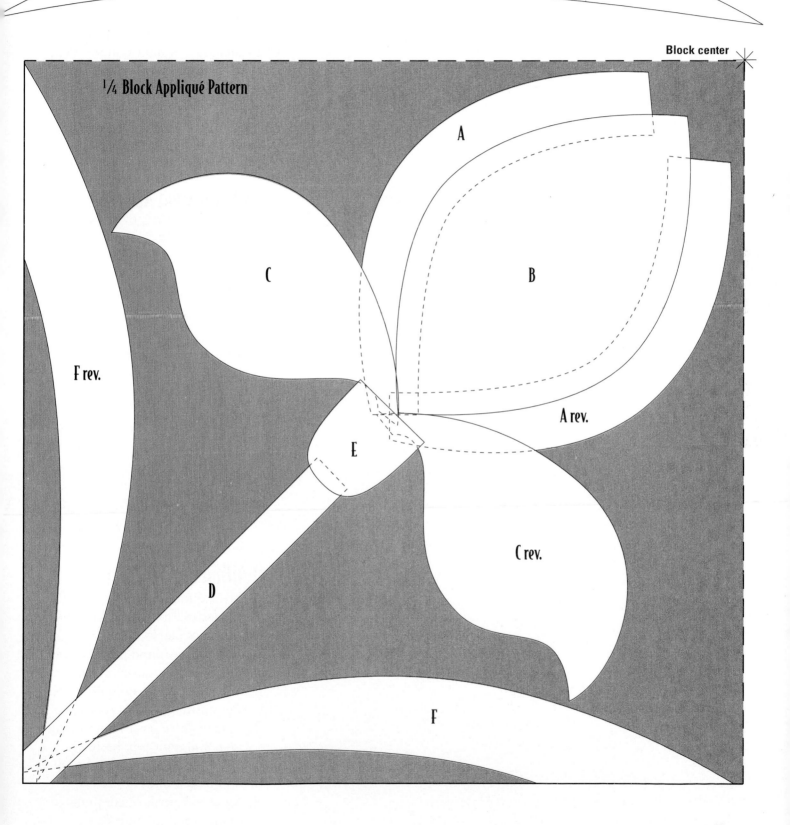

G

¼ Block Appliqué Pattern

A

C

B

F rev.

A rev.

E

C rev.

D

F

**½ Feathered Wreath
Quilting Pattern**

iris blocks and 1 row with yellow iris block.

3. For Row 3, lay out 2 appliquéd blocks, 1 plain block, and 2 plain half-blocks. Lay out 2 of Row 3.

4. Join blocks in each row.

5. Referring to photo, lay out rows in 1-2-3-2-3-2-1 order. Turn Row 1 upside down at quilt bottom. When satisfied with placement, join rows.

6. Measure length of quilt through middle. Trim light green border strips to match length. Sew borders to quilt sides, easing as necessary.

Leaf and Stem Appliqué

1. Fold each 1½" x 9" green strip in half, wrong sides facing. Stitch a ¼" seam, making a narrow tube. Slide each strip onto pressing bar, centering seam on flat side of bar. Press seam allowances open. Trim seam allowance if necessary.

2. Following traced guidelines on appliquéd blocks and half-blocks, position F and F reversed leaves over block seam lines. Substitute G and G reversed on half-blocks at outside edge. Pin stems over leaf ends, crossing where blocks meet. Pin Es over stem ends at bottom of each flower.

3. When satisfied with leaf and stem placement, appliqué.

Quilting and Finishing

1. Mark quilting designs on quilt top as desired. In addition to wreath on alternate blocks, quilt shown has echo quilting around flowers and leaves, spaced ½" apart. Borders have feathers and echo quilting. Use border quilting pattern on page 30.

2. Assemble backing. Layer backing, batting, and quilt top. Baste.

3. Outline-quilt appliqué. Add quilting as marked or as desired.

4. Make 9½ yards of continuous bias binding. Bind quilt edges.

Pomegranate

This is one of several Mountain Mist designs that makes
good use of orange, a popular color in the 1930s. Three red-orange
fruits bloom in perfect symmetry on each vine.
The fruit blocks alternate in a diagonal set with six rose blocks.

Quilt: 74" x 84"   **Blocks: 15 (14") squares**

Materials

5¾ yards white
2⅝ yards green
⅝ yard red-orange
⅜ yard dark green
⅜ yard red
¼ yard red dot
2¼ yards 90"-wide backing fabric
81" x 96" precut batting
¼"-wide bias pressing bar
14" square tracing paper

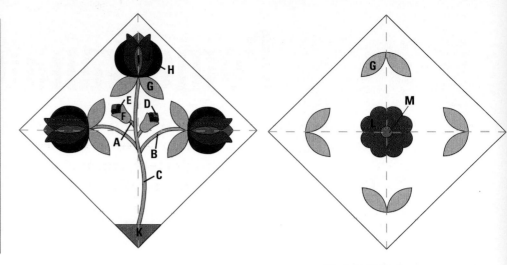

Block 1—Make 9.

Block 2—Make 6.

Cutting

Make templates for patterns D–M on pages 66 and 67. Add seam allowances to appliqué pieces when cutting. Cut pieces in order listed to make best use of yardage.

From white, cut:
• 4 (7½" x 88") lengthwise strips for border.
• 15 (14½") squares for blocks.
• 3 (21½") squares. Cut squares in quarters diagonally to get 11 setting triangles (and 1 extra).
• 1 (11") square. Cut square in half diagonally to get 2 corner triangles.

From green, cut:
• 36" square for binding.
• 4 (1½" x 94") lengthwise strips for sashing.
• 20 (1½" x 14½") sashing strips.
• 128 of Pattern G.
• 18 of Pattern F.

From red-orange, cut:
• 27 of Pattern H.
• 18 of Pattern E.
• 6 of Pattern L.

From red, cut:
• 27 of Pattern J.

From dark green, cut:
• 1 (9½" x 43") strip for A, B, and C stems.
• 9 of Pattern K.

From red dot, cut:
• 27 of Pattern I.
• 18 of Pattern D.
• 6 of Pattern M.

Making Blocks

See Quilt Smart Workshop, page 157, for tips on appliqué.

1. Fold and crease paper square to make placement guides **(Diagram A)**.
2. Align Pattern K seam lines with 1 corner of paper. Trace diagonal edge to mark bottom corner of block. Next, align opposite corner and placement line with top of pattern on page 67. Top of Pattern I (topmost tip of fruit) should be 1¾" below paper corner. Trace. Draw in remaining C stem down

to K triangle. Reposition paper over pattern to draw in 2 more pomegranates, centering each on placement line 1¾" from corner.
3. Fold and crease white fabric square to make placement guides.
4. Cut stems from dark green strip. First measure and rotary-cut a 3½" triangle off 1 end of strip to establish a 45° angle for bias cuts **(Diagram B)**. Measuring from *cut* edge, cut 1"-wide strips. Cut 9 (13¼"-long) C stems, 18 (5¾"-long) B stems, and 18 (1½"-long) A stems.
5. Follow Bias Appliqué instructions on page 73 to fold, stitch, and press bias strips on ¼"-wide pressing bar. Do not turn stem ends under, as these will be covered by other pieces.
6. Use pattern to position appliqué pieces in alphabetical order on fabric using one of these methods: a) place fabric square over pattern

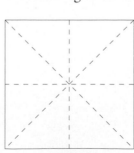

Diagram A

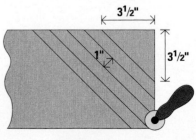

Diagram B

and use a nonpermanent marker to *lightly* trace design directly onto fabric;

b) tape traced pattern to a windowpane; then tape fabric over it and pin appliqué pieces in place;

c) position tracing on fabric and slide appliqués into position under it, pinning pieces in place.

7. When satisfied with placement, appliqué pieces in alphabetical order. Pin overlapping pieces out of the way to stitch down stems.

8. Appliqué 9 of Block 1.

9. For Block 2, center L and M pieces as shown in block diagram. Center a pair of G leaves on placement lines, 3½" from corner. Appliqué 6 of Block 2.

Quilt Assembly

Refer to photo on page 66 and Quilt Assembly Diagram *throughout.*

1. Lay out blocks in 5 diagonal rows as shown, alternating blocks 1 and 2. Place sashing strips between blocks. Each row ends with a triangle.

2. When satisfied with placement, join blocks, sashing strips, and triangles in each row. Press seam allowances toward sashing.

3. For Sashing Strip 1, cut 17" from a 94"-long green strip. Center this on long side of corner triangle and stitch. Then center sashing on side of Row 1 and stitch. Ends of sashing should extend beyond row at both ends.

4. For Sashing Strip 2, cut a 48"-long piece from same green strip. Center sashing on side of Row 2 as shown and stitch.

5. Center full-length green strips on sides of rows 3 and 4. Stitch.

6. From remaining green strip, cut a 61"-long piece for Sashing

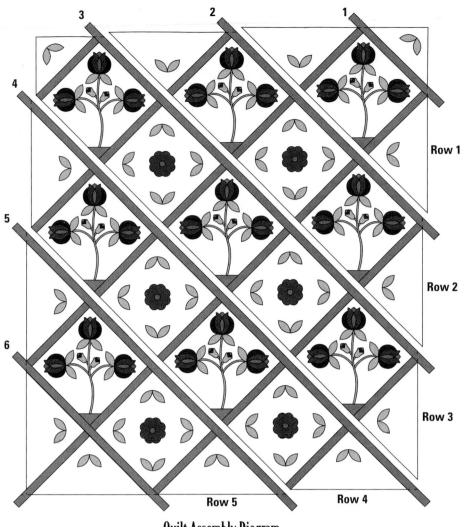

Quilt Assembly Diagram

Strip 5 and a 33"-long piece for Sashing Strip 6. Center these on opposite sides of Row 5; stitch.

7. From remaining green strip, cut a 17"-long piece for corner unit. Aligning ends, sew 2 setting triangles to sides of strip, letting strip extend at corner.

8. Align ruler with edge of each triangle, extending ruler over end of sashing (Diagram C). Trim sashing

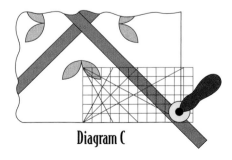

Diagram C

even with edge of triangle. Trim all sashing strips in same manner.

9. Join rows. Press seam allowances toward sashing strips.

10. Referring to photo, appliqué pairs of G leaves on each triangle, 3½" from corner.

Border

Quilt shown has borders of different widths. For ease of mitering and a more pleasing result, instructions are for borders of equal width.

See page 158 for tips on sewing a mitered border. Sew border strips to quilt and miter corners. *continued*

Dogwood

This is one of Phoebe Edwards's original designs. (See page 5 for more about Phoebe.) The simple white flower sparkles against a soft leaf-green background fabric, reminiscent of springtime blossoms. The quilt is an ideal size for a queen-size bed.

Quilt: 84" x 99"   **Blocks: 8 (15" x 25½") blocks**

Materials

6⅝ yards green*
3 yards brown
2⅛ yards white
⅜ yard yellow print
3 yards 90"-wide backing fabric
90" x 108" precut batting
¼"-wide bias pressing bar
*Note: A full 45"-width is needed to cut pieces. If yardage is narrower, you need 8 yards green.

Cutting

Make templates for patterns A, B, and C on page 76. Add seam allowances to appliqué pieces when cutting. Cut pieces in order listed to make best use of yardage.

From green, cut:
- 2 (17½" x 84") lengthwise strips for top and bottom borders.
- 2 (14½" x 99") lengthwise strips for side borders.
- 8 (15½" x 26") blocks.

From brown, cut:
- 4 (3" x 103") lengthwise strips for outer border.
- 30" x 36" piece for binding.
- 3 (7½" x 30") strips for stems.
- 708 of Pattern B.

From white, cut:
- 177 of Pattern A.

From yellow, cut:
- 177 of Pattern C.

Making Blocks

See Quilt Smart Workshop, page 157, for tips on appliqué.

1. Fold and crease a green block to make placement guides (Diagram A).
2. Center an A flower on block, aligning top of each heart-shaped petal with a center crease.
3. Referring to block diagram, pin 13 flowers on block, centering each piece on diagonal placement lines. (Flowers at block corners are appliquéd over seams *after* blocks are joined.) Appliqué.
4. Appliqué Bs and Cs on flowers, completing 4 blocks as shown.
5. For partial blocks, appliqué 10 flowers as shown. Make 2 blocks with upper right corner empty and 2 blocks with upper left corner empty. *continued*

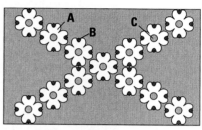

Dogwood Block–Make 4.

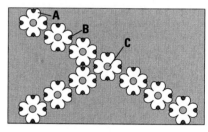

Partial Block–Make 2.

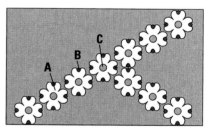

Partial Block–Make 2.

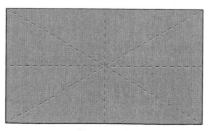

Diagram A

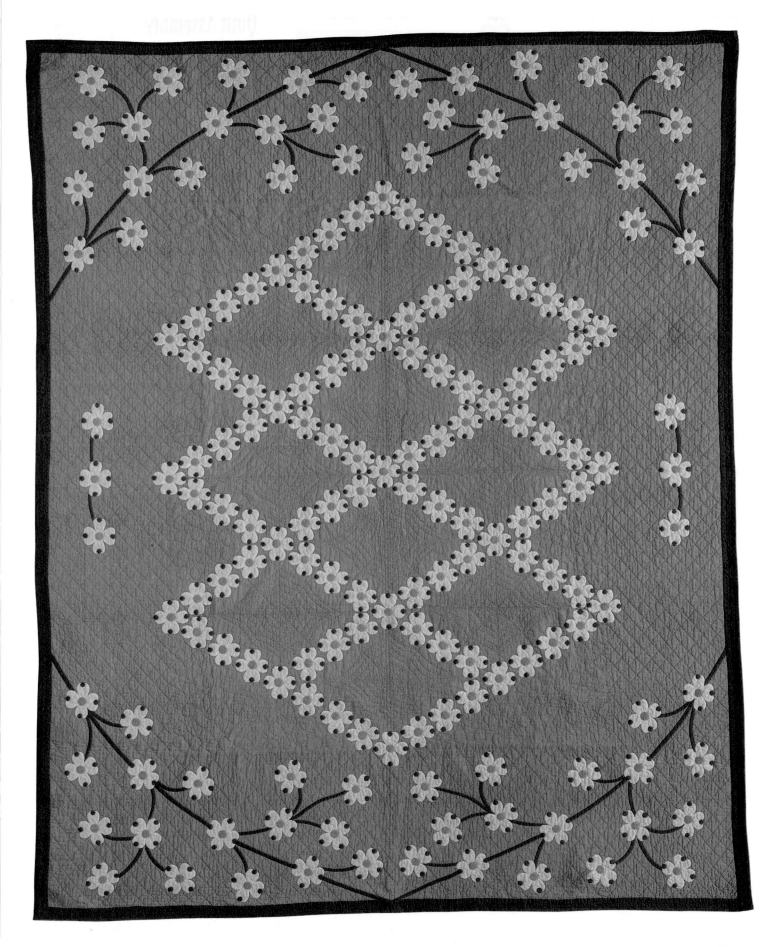

Trumpet Vines

This graceful appliqué celebrates the trumpet flower, a fragrant wildflower native to the southeastern states. The quilt's vines grow in symmetrical clusters, making an elegant display of bright blossoms.

Quilt: 81" x 97"   **Blocks: 4 (24" x 32") blocks**

Materials

6 yards white
2¾ yards green
⅜ yard red-orange
¼ yard tangerine
⅛ yard peach
2⅞ yards 90"-wide backing fabric
90" x 108" precut batting
Tracing paper and pencil
¼"-wide bias pressing bar

Cutting

Make templates for patterns A, B, C, D, E, F, G, and J on pages 82 and 83. Add seam allowances to appliqué pieces when cutting. Cut pieces in order listed to make best use of yardage.

From white, cut:
- 4 (24½" x 32½") pieces for blocks.
- 2 (17" x 65") lengthwise strips and 2 (17" x 83") lengthwise strips for border.

From green, cut:
- 36" square for binding.
- 2 (10"-wide) cross-grain strips for bias stems H and I.
- 336 of Pattern G.
- 24 of Pattern D.
- 24 of Pattern D reversed.
- 12 of Pattern E.
- 12 of Pattern E reversed.
- 9 of Pattern J.

From red-orange, cut:
- 72 of Pattern B.

From tangerine, cut:
- 12 of Pattern C.
- 12 of Pattern C reversed.

From peach, cut:
- 24 of Pattern A.
- 12 of Pattern F.
- 12 of Pattern F reversed.

Making Blocks

See Quilt Smart Workshop, page 157, for tips on appliqué.

1. Cut stems from 10"-wide green strips. First measure and rotary-cut a 4¼" triangle off end of strip to establish a 45° angle for bias cuts **(Diagram A)**. Measuring from *cut* edge, cut 1"-wide strips. Cut 24 (14"-long) I stems and 48 (5"-long) H stems.

2. Follow Bias Appliqué instructions on page 73 to fold, stitch, and press each bias strip on pressing bar. Do not turn stem ends under, as these are covered by other pieces.

3. Cut a 12¼" x 16¼" piece of tracing paper. Measure and mark 2" from bottom left corner of paper; then draw a line to connect points, drawing a triangle at each corner **(Diagram B)**. This is placement line for J. Using measurements shown, draw a 5" x 5½" box near top right corner of paper.

4. Align drawn box on paper with boxed portion of pattern on page 83. Trace pattern. Extend lines of I stem down to corner triangle. Traced pattern is ¼ of block. Darken tracing on both sides of tracing paper.

5. With pattern right side up, align bottom left corner of fabric rectangle with corner of pattern. Use a nonpermanent marker to *lightly* trace design on fabric. Flip pattern over to mark second G/H branch. Repeat for top right corner. Then turn pattern wrong side up to trace design in bottom right and top left corners to get mirror-image clusters that arch toward center of block.

6. Use markings to align prepared I stems at each corner of fabric rectangle. Position Es, Gs, and H stems. When satisfied with

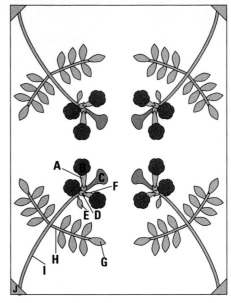

Trumpet Vines Block—Make 4.

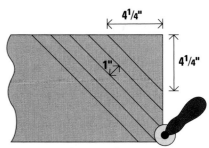

Diagram A

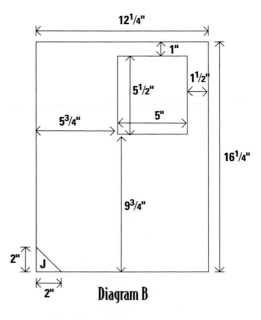

Diagram B

placement, appliqué each G/H branch, pinning I stems out of the way as you stitch. Sew E leaves in place; then stitch I stems.

continued

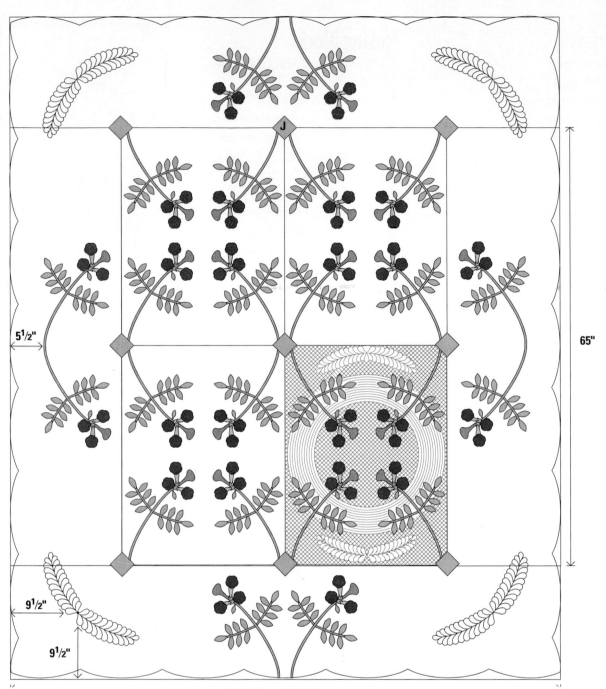

5½"

65"

9½"

9½"

Quilt Assembly Diagram

7. Pin A, B, C, D, and F pieces in place. When satisfied with placement, appliqué pieces in place. Pin overlapping pieces out of the way to stitch down A, C, and F.
8. Appliqué 4 corners of block in same manner. Use reversed pieces for clusters in top left and lower right corners of block.
9. Make 4 blocks.

Appliquéing Borders
1. Fold each border strip in half and mark center of 1 long edge with a pin.
2. On each 83"-long strip, match ends of 2 I stems with edge of border about ½" on each side of center point and pin stems in place. Trace pattern, right side up, to mark flower cluster on right stem. Turn pattern over,

facedown, to trace flower cluster on left stem. Pin pieces in place as shown **(Quilt Assembly Diagram)**. When satisfied with placement, appliqué pieces in place on each strip.
3. On each 65"-long side border strip, measure 5½" from bottom center and mark point where 2 stems will meet. With pattern right side up, trace stem and flower cluster to right of center.

Turn pattern facedown to trace left stem and flowers. Pin pieces in place. When satisfied with placement, appliqué pieces in place on each strip.

Quilt Assembly

Refer to photo and Quilt Assembly Diagram *throughout.*

1. Lay out blocks in rows, with 2 blocks in each row. Join blocks in each row.

2. Join rows as shown.

3. Measure length of joined blocks; then trim side borders to match length, trimming equal amounts from each end of border. Matching centers, sew borders to quilt sides. Press seam allowances toward borders.

4. Measure width of quilt; trim remaining borders to match quilt width. Sew borders to top and bottom edges of quilt.

5. Turn under edges of each J square. Center a square at corner of each block, centering J corners on seams. Appliqué 9 J squares in place as shown.

Quilting and Finishing

Quilt Assembly Diagram shows quilting design of quilt shown. Follow steps 1–4 to mark quilt like this, if desired, or choose your own quilting design. If scalloped edge is desired, do not cut scallops until quilting is complete.

1. Make a tracing of Feather Quilting Pattern on page 82. Darken drawing on both sides of paper. Tape tracing onto a light box or a bright windowpane. Center each block on pattern, aligning middle of block with center line of pattern. Lightly trace design onto fabric. Turn pattern over to trace second side of design. Trace feather pattern at top and bottom of each block.

2. Measure 9½" from each border corner to mark center point of corner feathers. Mark quilting pattern on border corners.

3. Starting at ends of G/H stems, mark concentric circles around block design. Mark 11 circles, spaced ⅜" apart.

4. Use a ruler to lightly mark diagonal cross-hatching on remaining areas of quilt, spacing lines ½" apart.

5. Layer backing, batting, and quilt top. Baste.

6. Outline-quilt appliqués as shown. Add more quilting as marked or as desired.

7. If scalloped edge is desired, make a template of designated portion of quilting pattern's spine. This is ½ of a scallop. Match center of scallop with center of each side of quilt and mark scallops along each border, turning template over to trace second half of each scallop. Trim borders.

8. Make 10⅛ yards of bias binding for a straight-edged quilt or 11 yards for a scalloped edge. Bind quilt edges.

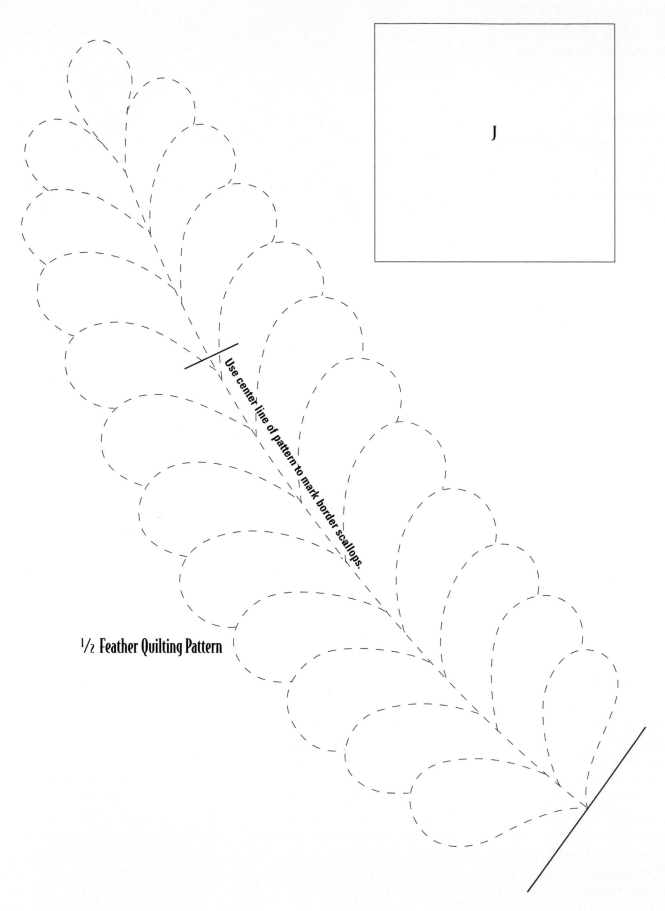

J

Use center line of pattern to mark border scallops.

½ Feather Quilting Pattern

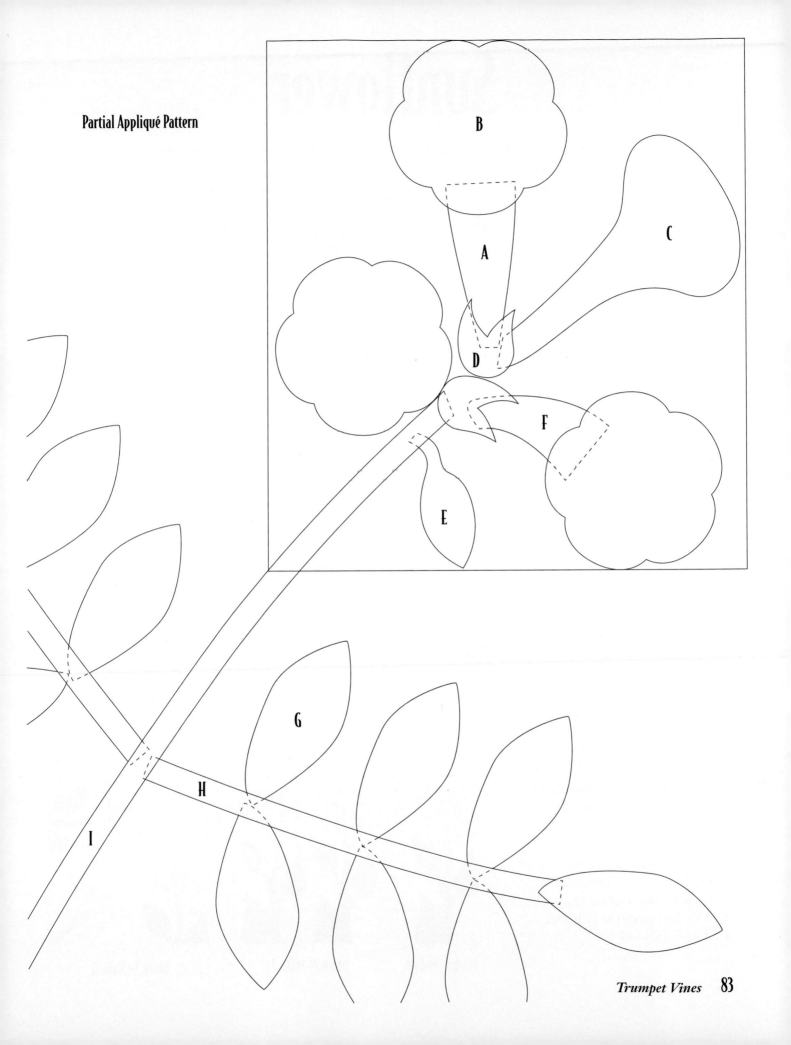

Partial Appliqué Pattern

B

C

A

D

F

E

G

H

I

Sunflower

These cheerful sunflowers capture summertime's golden glow. An early Mountain Mist pattern, this is one of several floral designs created by Margaret Hayes of Knoxville.

Finished Size: 81" x 98"

**Blocks: 6 (12" x 22") blocks
2 (19" x 22") blocks
4 (22") squares**

Materials

4 yards cream or muslin
3 yards brown
3 yards green
2½ yards yellow
3 yards 90"-wide backing fabric
90" x 108" precut batting
Tracing paper and pencil

Cutting

Make templates for patterns A–H on pages 87, 88, and 89. See instructions at right on making a complete pattern. Use complete pattern to make templates for A stem and C leaf. Add seam allowances to appliqué pieces when cutting. Cut pieces in order listed to make best use of yardage.

From cream, cut:
- 4 (22½") squares for Block 3.
- 2 (19½" x 22½") Block 2 pieces.
- 19½" x 36½" piece for center.
- 6 (12½" x 22½") Block 1 pieces.

From brown, cut:
- 2 (4½" x 104") lengthwise strips and 2 (4½" x 87") lengthwise strips for outer borders.
- 25" x 36" piece for binding.
- 22 of Pattern H.

From green, cut:
- 10 (4½" x 44") cross-grain strips for middle borders.
- 10 of whole Pattern A.
- 8 of partial Pattern A for Block 3.
- 4 of partial Pattern A for corner flower, Block 3.
- 18 of Pattern B.
- 10 of whole Pattern C.
- 8 of partial Pattern C for Block 3.
- 10 of Pattern D.

From yellow, cut:
- 10 (4½" x 44") cross-grain strips for middle borders.
- 44 of Pattern E.
- 44 of Pattern E reversed.
- 110 of Pattern F.
- 22 of Pattern F reversed.
- 66 of Pattern G.

Making a Pattern

Appliqué is easier if you work with a complete tracing of the design. When appliqué is complete, save the pattern to use later to make a quilting stencil.

1. Tape pieces of tracing paper together to make a paper rectangle 21" long.

2. Center paper over Section 1 pattern on page 87, aligning end of paper with bottom of Pattern D. Trace pattern. Include markings for underlap on leaves and stem.

3. Center paper over Section 2 pattern on page 88, aligning Section 1 drawing with overlap indicated on pattern. Trace Section 2, including dotted cutting lines for Block 3 stems.

4. Trace Section 3 to complete pattern. *continued*

Block 1–Make 6.

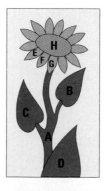

Block 2–Make 2.

Block 3–Make 4.

5. Use complete pattern to position appliqué pieces on blocks using one of these methods:
a) center fabric over pattern and use a nonpermanent marker to *lightly* trace design on fabric;
b) tape pattern to a windowpane; then tape fabric over it and pin appliqué pieces in place;
c) center pattern over fabric and slide appliqués into position under it, pinning pieces in place.

Making Blocks

See Quilt Smart Workshop, page 157, for tips on appliqué.

1. For Block 1, center A stem on a 12½" x 22½" block. Then place B, C, and D leaves. Leaf D should align with bottom edge of block. (Do not turn under bottom edge of D, as this is sewn into seam when borders are joined.) When satisfied with position, appliqué pieces in place, pinning leaves out of the way to work on stem.

2. Pin E, F, and G petals in place; then position H piece over ends of petals. When satisfied with placement, appliqué flower pieces in place to complete block.

3. Make 6 of Block 1.

4. Make Block 2 in same manner, placing 2 flowers on 19½"-wide block as shown. Petals and leaves of flowers will be close but should not touch. Make 2 of Block 2.

5. For Block 3, position shortest stem at corner; then pin petals and H center at top of stem. At sides, pin medium-length stems and leaves as shown. Be sure pieces do not extend into seam allowances where block will be sewn to adjacent block. When satisfied with placement of all pieces, appliqué. Make 4 of Block 3.

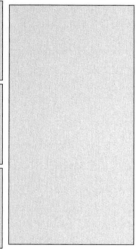

Quilt Assembly Diagram

Quilt Assembly

Refer to photo and **Quilt Assembly Diagram** *throughout.*

1. Join 3 of Block 1 in a row; then sew row to 1 side of center panel. Repeat for opposite side. Be sure heads of flowers are against center panel. Press seam allowances toward center.

2. Sew a Block 3 to both sides of each Block 2. Press seam allowances toward corner blocks. Sew these rows to top and bottom of center panel as shown.

Borders

1. Join 3 green strips end-to-end to make each side border and join 2 green strips each for top and bottom borders. Repeat with yellow strips.

2. Sew green and brown strips to opposite sides of each yellow strip. Make 2 (104"-long) side borders and 2 (87"-long) end borders. Press seam allowances toward green.

3. See page 158 for tips on sewing a mitered border. Sew border strips to center section and miter corners.

Quilting and Finishing

1. Mark quilting design on quilt top as desired. To quilt your quilt top as shown, make a stencil of paper pattern. Or, if you prefer, position quilt top over drawing and trace design. Mark leaves and flowers between sunflowers as desired. For center section, mark an oval of flower petals; then fill center with diagonal lines of cross-hatching, spaced 1" apart. Repeat cross-hatching in borders.

2. Layer backing, batting, and quilt top. Baste.

3. Outline-quilt appliqué. Add additional quilting as desired or as marked.

4. Make 10¼ yards of continuous bias binding. Bind quilt edges.

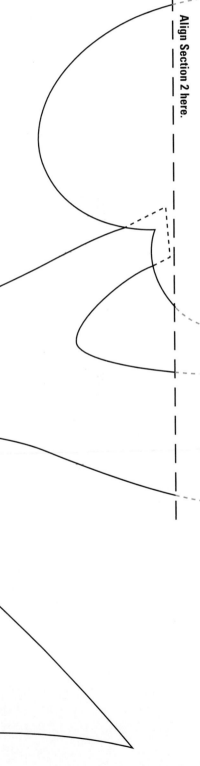

Section 1

Align Section 2 here.

D

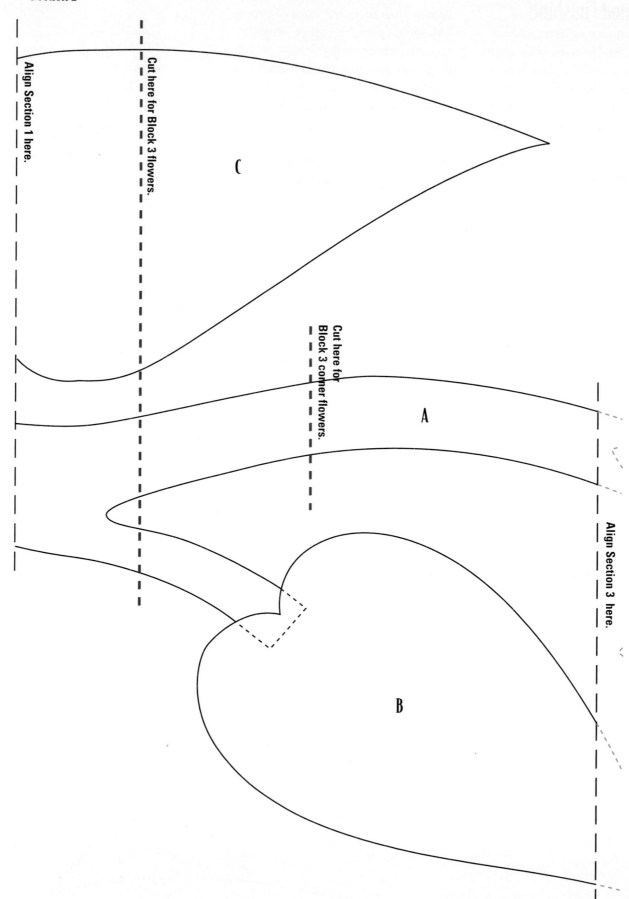

Align Section 1 here.

Cut here for Block 3 flowers.

C

Cut here for Block 3 corner flowers.

A

Align Section 3 here.

B

F

G

E

E
rev.

E

F

F

G

H

F

F

E

F
rev.

E
rev.

G

F

The Pleasures of Patchwork

"Piecin' a quilt's like livin' a life . . . The Lord sends us the pieces, but we cut 'em out and put 'em together to suit ourselves, and there's a heap more in the cuttin' and the sewin' than there is in the calico."

Aunt Jane of Kentucky, 1900

Country Lanes

Tumbling Blocks

The first of the Mountain Mist quilt patterns, this 1930s quilt features diamonds and triangles in white and three pink fabrics (a solid and two prints). We've restructured the piecing a bit to reduce the number of set-in seams needed.

Quilt: 72" x 90"   Blocks: 152 (9"-wide x 4½"-high) blocks

Materials

4¼ yards white or muslin
2½ yards pink solid
1¼ yards pink print
1¼ yards pink-on-white print
5½ yards backing fabric
81" x 96" precut batting

Cutting

Instructions are for rotary cutting. **Cut all strips cross-grain,** from selvage to selvage. For traditional piecing, use patterns on pages 95 and 96.

From white, cut:
- 20 (3"-wide) strips. Cut 20 Cs and 2 Es (or E reversed) triangles from each strip to get a total of 480 Cs, 20 Es, and 20 Es reversed.
- 13 (5"-wide) strips. From these, cut 66 Ds and 20 Fs.
- 2 (2¾"-wide) strips. From these, cut 8 of Pattern G.

From pink solid, cut:
- 34" square for binding.
- 14 (3"-wide) strips. From these, cut 152 Bs and 16 Cs.

From pink print and white print, cut:
- 160 A diamonds of *each* fabric.

Making Blocks

See page 143 for tips on sewing set-in seams.

1. To begin Block 1, join pink print and white print A diamonds as shown **(Block 1 Diagram).**

2. Set-in B (see tip box on page 143 for more on sewing set-in seams). Press seam allowances away from B.

3. Sew C triangles to ends of block as shown. Press seam allowances toward Cs.

4. For Block 2, join pink print and white print A diamonds in same manner, changing position of diamonds as shown **(Block 2 Diagram).** Repeat steps 2 and 3 to complete block.

5. Make 76 of Block 1 and 76 of Block 2.

Making Other Units

1. For Unit 3, sew C triangles to opposite sides of each D piece **(Unit 3 Diagram).** Make 66 of Unit 3. Press seam allowances toward Cs.

2. For Unit 4, join A diamonds and pink solid C triangles **(Unit 4 Diagram).** Make 4 units with pink print diamonds and 4 units with white print diamonds. Sew white Cs to both ends of each unit as shown.

3. For Unit 5, join A diamonds and pink solid C triangles **(Unit 5 Diagram).** Sew a white C triangle to pink triangle as shown. Make 4 of Unit 5 with pink print diamonds and 4 units with white diamonds.

continued

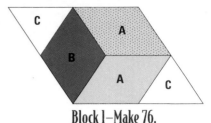

Block 1–Make 76.

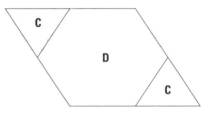

Block 2–Make 76.

Unit 3–Make 66.

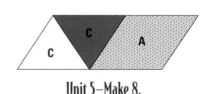

Unit 4–Make 8.

Unit 5–Make 8.

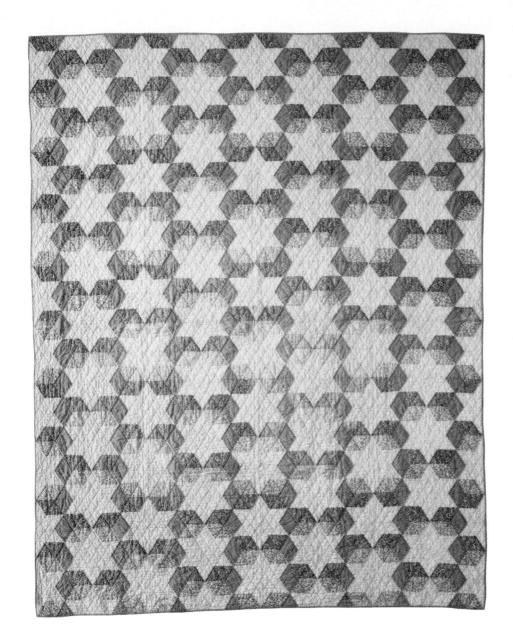

Quilt Assembly

Refer to photo and Row Assembly Diagram throughout. In row assembly, press seam allowances toward white C triangles.

1. For Row 1, select 4 each of units 4 and 5, 4 Gs, and 1 each of E and E reversed. Remove white C triangle from 1 Unit 4 (indicated as 4x on diagram). Replace it with E triangle as shown.

2. Join units in a row as shown. Make first Row 1 with pink print units and second Row 1 with white print units.

3. For Row 2, join a white C triangle to a short leg of each F as shown.

4. For each Row 2, join 4 each of units 1 and 2, 3 of Unit 3, and 2 F/G units as shown. Make 10 of Row 2.

5. For Row 3, join 4 each of units 1, 2, and 3 as shown. At ends of row, remove last C triangles; then sew Es and Es reversed to end units as shown. Make 9 of Row 3.

6. Lay out rows to check placement. Start with Row 1 and then alternate rows 2 and 3. Place remaining Row 1 at bottom, turning it upside down.

7. When satisfied with layout, join rows to complete quilt top.

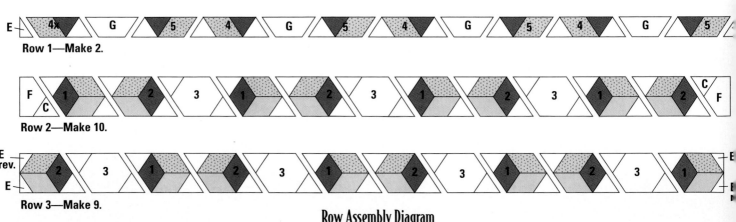

E

Row 1—Make 2.

Row 2—Make 10.

E rev.

E

Row 3—Make 9.

Row Assembly Diagram

Quilting and Finishing

1. Mark quilting design on quilt top as desired. Quilt shown is outline-quilted with diagonal cross-hatching (spaced 1" apart) quilted in D pieces.

2. Assemble backing. Layer backing, batting, and quilt top. Baste.

3. Quilt as desired.

4. Make 9½ yards of continuous bias binding. Bind quilt edges.

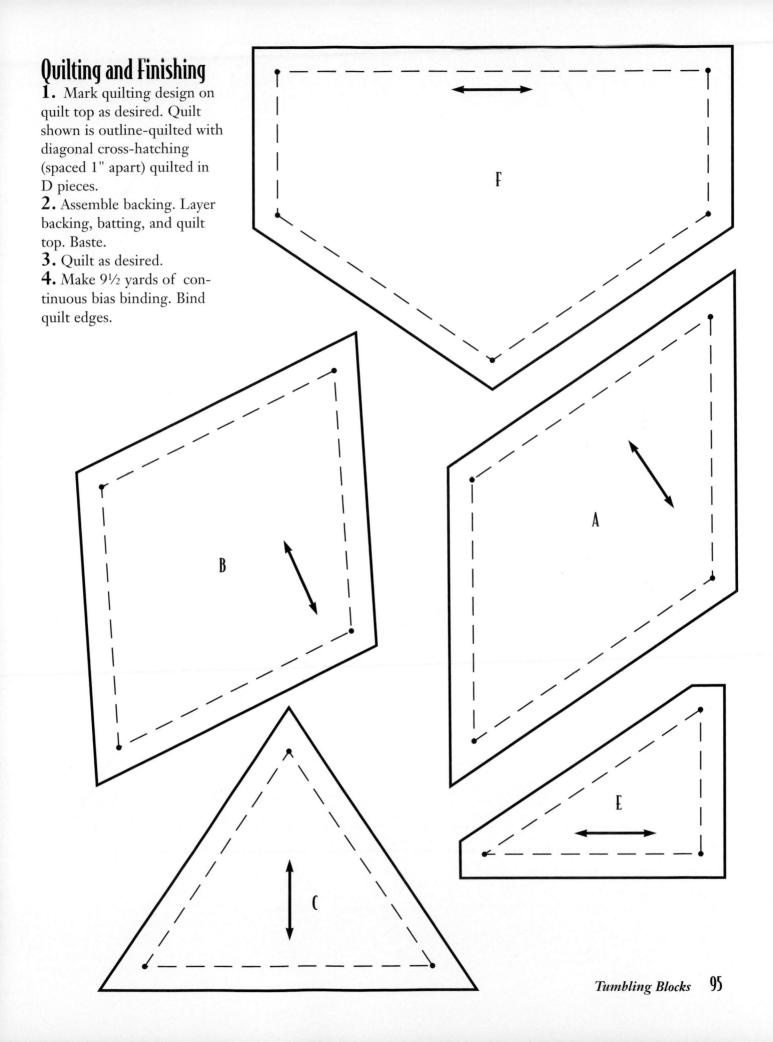

Tumbling Blocks **95**

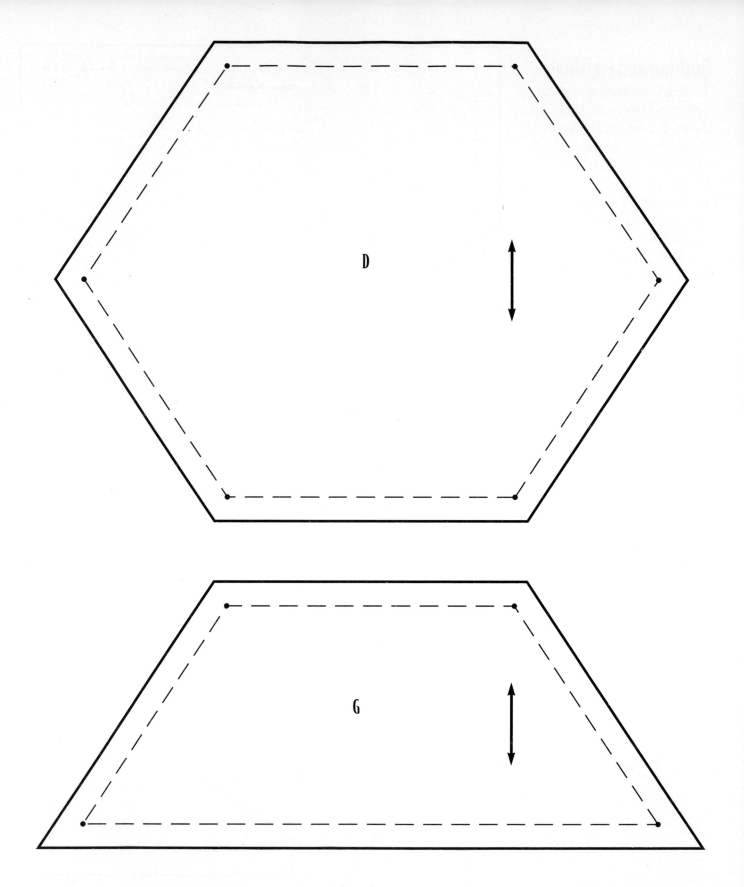

D

G

Boston Commons

This pattern is ideal for quick cutting and piecing. Our instructions introduce you to Seminole patchwork, a strip-piecing technique invented by Seminole Indians who use it to make festive costumes. Give your rotary cutter a real workout with this scrap-lover's delight.

Quilt: 88" x 103½"

Materials

6 yards muslin
34 (3" x 18") strips assorted prints
1 yard binding fabric
2⅝ yards 108"-wide backing fabric
120" x 120" precut batting
Rotary cutter and acrylic ruler
Zip-top plastic storage bags
    (optional)

Cutting

These instructions are for rotary cutting. For traditional piecing, use patterns on page 100.

Seminole Patchwork eliminates the need to cut individual squares and triangles. Instead, you'll use strips, which are sewn into sets. These strip sets are cut into segments for further piecing. So there's no need to cut scrap strips further until strip sets are made.

From muslin, cut:
• 2 (8½" x 90") and 2 (2½" x 90") lengthwise strips for outer border.
• 4 (7½" x 74") lengthwise strips for middle border.
• 4 (8½" x 37") cross-grain strips for inner border.
• 2 (3" x 42") cross-grain strips for piecing.
• 47 (3" x 18") strips for strip sets.

Center Section

Refer to **Strip Set Diagrams** *throughout.*

1. Join 4 scrap strips as shown to make Strip Set 1. Press seam allowances in 1 direction, indicated by arrow on diagram. Make 4 of Strip Set 1, using different fabrics in each set.

2. Throughout these instructions, **cut all segments 3" wide.** From *each* Strip Set 1, cut 1 segment.

Join these to make center square **(Diagram A).** Numbers on diagram indicate strip sets. Turn adjacent units upside down as needed to get offset seam allowances. (Set aside remainder of Strip Set 1 for Strip Set 6.)

3. Join scrap strips to make 6 of Strip Set 2 and 5 of Strip Set 3. Press seam allowances in directions of arrows shown.

4. From Strip Set 2, cut 32 segments. From Strip Set 3, cut 28 segments. To keep segments tidy until needed, store each set in a zig-top bag. Label each bag with appropriate strip-set number.

5. Select 8 Strip Set 2 segments and 4 Set 3 segments. Sew a #2 segment to both sides of each #3.

6. From muslin strip, cut 6 (3") squares. Sew squares to sides of 2/3 units as shown **(Diagram A).** Numbers on diagram identify strip-set segments.

7. Sew 2/3 units with 1 muslin square to sides of center unit as shown. Sew remaining units to top and bottom edges.

8. To trim ragged edges of unit, use acrylic ruler to measure ¼" from corners of print squares **(Diagram B).** Be sure ruler is correctly aligned with each corner along the cutting line so you are sure to cut a straight edge. Trim edges on all sides to complete center unit.

9. See page 158 for tips on sewing a mitered border. Sew 37"-long border strips to center section and miter corners **(Quilt Assembly Diagram).**

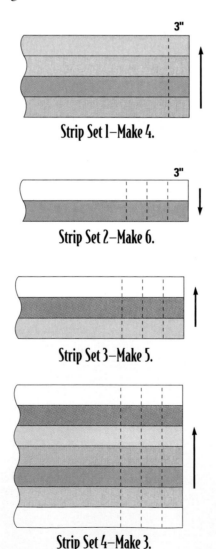

3"

Strip Set 1–Make 4.

3"

Strip Set 2–Make 6.

Strip Set 3–Make 5.

Strip Set 4–Make 3.

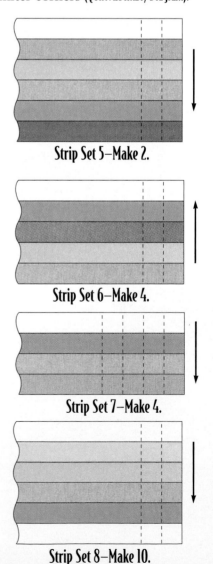

Strip Set 5–Make 2.

Strip Set 6–Make 4.

Strip Set 7–Make 4.

Strip Set 8–Make 10.

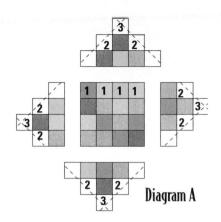

Diagram A

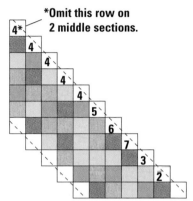

Diagram B

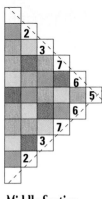

Diagram C

Middle Section
Corner–Make 4.

*Omit this row on
2 middle sections.

Middle Section–Make 4.

Middle Section

1. Referring to Strip Set Diagrams, make 3 of Strip Set 4, 2 of Strip Set 5, and 4 of Strip Set 7. Sew a muslin strip to each Strip Set 1 remnant to make 4 of Strip Set 6. Press seam allowances in directions indicated by arrows.

2. Cut 18 segments from Set 4, 8 segments from Set 5, 20 segments from Set 6, and 24 segments from Set 7. Cut 4 (3") squares from muslin strip.

3. Select segments to make Middle Section as shown. Numbers on diagram identify strip-set segments. With right sides facing, align *seams* of first 2 segments, offsetting top and bottom edges (Diagram C). Turn units upside down as needed to offset seam allowances. Stitch. Check seam alignment on right side. Chain-sew pairs in this way; then join pairs to complete Middle Section. Make 2 sections as shown; then make 2 more sections *omitting* first #4 segment.

4. Make 4 Middle Section Corner Units as shown.

5. Press all Middle units; then trim ragged edges. Mark centers on each Middle Section.

6. Match marked center on each longer Middle Section with center of side inner borders and stitch (Quilt Assembly Diagram).

7. Match centers of remaining (shorter) Middle Sections to centers of top and bottom inner borders. Stitch, sewing across corners of side sections. Trim excess seam allowance at corners.

8. Sew Middle Section Corners to quilt (outlined in red on assembly diagram).

9. Sew 74"-long border strips to quilt edges and miter corners.

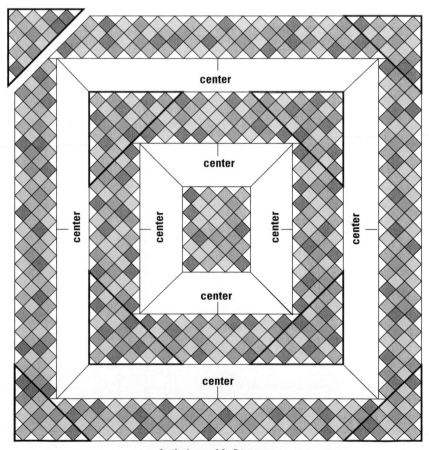

Quilt Assembly Diagram

Outer Section

1. Make 10 of Strip Set 8. Press seam allowances in direction indicated. Cut 62 segments. (If able to cut only 60 segments from strip sets, make 2 more from leftovers of previous strip sets.) Cut 4 (3") muslin squares.

2. Select segments to make Outer Section as shown. Aligning seams as before, chain-sew segment pairs. Join pairs to complete Outer Section. Make 2 Outer Sections as shown; then make 2 sections omitting first #8 segment.

3. Make 4 Outer Section Corner Units as shown.

4. Press all Outer units; then trim ragged edges. Mark centers on each section.

5. Match marked center on each longer Outer Section with center of muslin side borders and stitch (Quilt Assembly Diagram).

6. Match centers of remaining (shorter) Outer Sections to centers of top and bottom borders. Stitch, sewing across corners of side sections. Trim excess seam allowance at corners.

7. Sew Outer Corners to quilt.

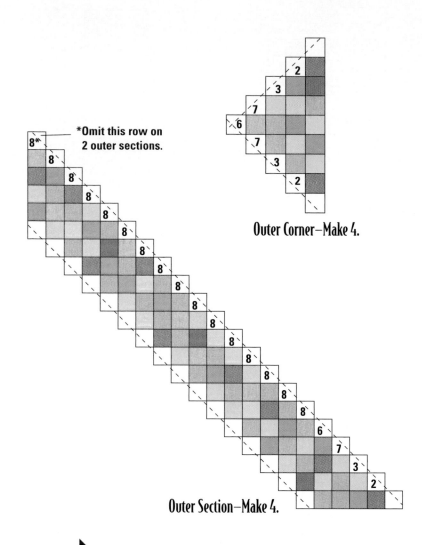

Outer Corner–Make 4.

*Omit this row on 2 outer sections.

Outer Section–Make 4.

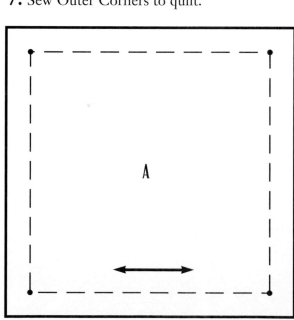

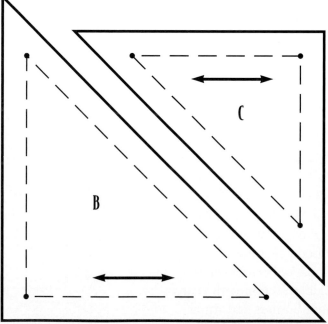

A

B

C

Borders

1. Measure length of quilt; then trim 2½"-wide muslin borders to match quilt length. Sew borders to quilt sides. Press seam allowances toward borders.
2. Measure width of quilt. Trim 8½"-wide muslin strips to match quilt width. Sew borders to top and bottom edges of quilt.

Quilting and Finishing

1. Mark quilting design on quilt top as desired. On quilt shown, patchwork is outline-quilted and a feather design is quilted in borders with diagonal cross-hatching (spaced ½" apart) surrounding feathers. For a feather pattern, enlarge pattern on page 30 by 150% on a photocopy machine.

2. Layer backing, batting, and quilt top. Baste.
3. Quilt as desired.
4. Cut a 34" square from binding fabric. Make 11 yards of continuous bias binding. Bind quilt edges.

Bed of Peonies

Complementary red and green on a white field make this traditional design even more of a classic. The color scheme and the sideways setting of the blocks is typical of nineteenth-century quilts.

Quilt: 85" x 102"   **Blocks: 20 (12") squares**

Materials

6 yards white or muslin
4¾ yards green
1¼ yards red
3⅛ yards 90"-wide backing fabric
90" x 108" precut batting
⅜"-wide bias pressing bar

Cutting

For traditional cutting, make templates of patterns A–D on page 105. For appliqué, make templates of patterns E and F. Add seam allowances when cutting appliqué pieces. Cut pieces in order listed to make best use of yardage.

From white, cut:
- 2 (6" x 90") and 2 (6" x 84") lengthwise strips for middle border.
- 4 (18¼") squares. Cut squares in quarters diagonally to get 14 setting triangles (and 2 extra).
- 2 (9½") squares. Cut squares in half diagonally to get 4 corner triangles.
- 12 (12½") setting squares.
- 20 (6½") D squares.
- 60 (4") squares. Cut squares in quarters diagonally to get 240 C triangles.
- 240 (2¼") B squares.

From green, cut:
- 32" square for binding.
- 4 (2½" x 100") lengthwise strips and 4 (1½" x 90") lengthwise strips for borders.
- 5 (7½" x 27") strips for bias stems.
- 5 (4") squares. Cut each square in quarters diagonally to get 20 C triangles.
- 20 of Pattern E.
- 20 of Pattern F.
- 10 (1¾" x 27") strips. From these, cut 120 A diamonds.

From red, cut:
- 12 (1¾"-wide) cross-grain strips. From these, cut 360 A diamonds.

Making Blocks

See Quilt Smart Workshop, pages 156–158, for tips on piecing and appliqué. See page 143 for tips on sewing a set-in seam.

1. Join diamonds in pairs as shown **(Diagram A)**. Press joining seam allowances open. Set a triangle into opening of each pair.

2. Join 2 diamond pairs. Set a square into each new opening.

3. Join halves. Press seam allowance open. Set remaining squares into open corners.

4. Make 3 flower units. Join these and D square in rows, positioning flowers as shown **(Block Assembly Diagram)**. Join rows.   *continued*

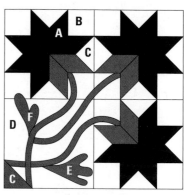

Peony Block—Make 20.

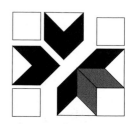

Diagram A

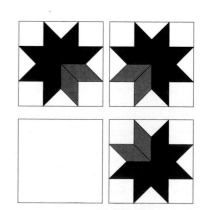

Block Assembly Diagram

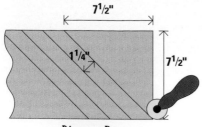

Diagram B

Diagram C

5. Cut stems from 7½"-wide green strips. First measure and rotary-cut a 7½" triangle from end of strip to establish 45° angle **(Diagram B)**. Measuring from *cut* edge, cut 1¼"-wide strips. Each strip is 10½" long. Cut 60 stems, 3 for each block. Follow Bias Appliqué instructions on page 73 to prepare strips on pressing bar.

6. Lay block corner over D pattern on page 105. Lightly trace position of leaves and stems on fabric. Pin E and F in place.

7. To make a point at 1 end of each stem, turn corners to wrong side **(Diagram C)**. Press. Trim seam allowances to make point lay flat.

8. Pin stem point at bottom of each flower. Pin stems, following placement lines on D square.

9. Pin green C triangle at corner of block, matching corner edges and covering stem ends. Turn under seam allowance on diagonal edge of triangle; press.

10. When satisfied with position of leaves and stems, appliqué. Stitch E and F leaves; then sew stems, moving C aside. Stitch C over stem ends. Press.

11. Trim D corner under C triangle, leaving ¼" seam allowance.

12. Make 20 Peony blocks.

Quilt Assembly

Refer to Quilt Assembly Diagram *throughout.*

1. Quilt is joined in 8 diagonal rows. For each row, lay out blocks and setting squares as shown, ending row with a setting triangle and/or corner triangle. Position flowers as shown or as desired.

2. When satisfied with layout, join blocks in each row. Press seam allowances toward setting squares and triangles.

3. Join rows.

Borders

1. Measure length of quilt; then trim 2 (1½" x 90") green borders to match quilt length. Sew borders to quilt sides.

2. Measure width of quilt. Trim remaining 1½"-wide green strip to match quilt width. Sew borders to top and bottom edges of quilt.

3. Repeat steps 1 and 2 to add white borders. Add remaining green borders in same manner.

Quilting and Finishing

1. Mark quilting design on quilt top as desired. Quilt shown is outline-quilted with ferns and feathered wreaths quilted in setting squares. See page 35 for a feathered wreath pattern—enlarge pattern on a photocopy machine to 130% to fit this quilt.

2. Layer backing, batting, and quilt top. Baste.

3. Quilt as marked or as desired.

4. Make 10¾ yards of continuous bias binding. Bind quilt edges.

Quilt Assembly Diagram

Shadow Trail

The clean, crisp look of solid-colored fabrics is ideal for this quilt's play on pattern and line. You'll find patterns for traditional piecing, but we recommend the strip-piecing techniques that make today's quiltmaking fast and fun.

Quilt: 92" x 98"

Materials

5¾ yards white or muslin
2¾ yards dark blue
2⅛ yards green
¾ yard light blue
3 yards 108"-wide backing fabric
120" x 120" precut batting
Rotary cutter and acrylic ruler
Zip-top plastic storage bags
    (optional)

Cutting

Instructions are for rotary cutting. For traditional piecing, use patterns on pages 109 and 111.

Strip-piecing eliminates the need to cut individual diamonds and stripes. Instead, you sew strips into sets, which are cut into segments for further piecing. Cut all strips cross-grain unless otherwise indicated.

From white, cut:
- 39 (2½"-wide) strips for strip sets.
- 2 (3½" x 81") and 2 (2½" x 85") lengthwise strips for side borders.
- 2 (3½" x 66") and 1 (2½" x 66") lengthwise strips for end borders.
- 2 (8½") squares (G) for middle border.
- 2 (6½") squares (H) for outer border.
- 6 of Pattern E.
- 6 of Pattern E reversed.
- 21 (3½" x 24") strips and 5 (3½" x 43") strips. From these, cut 118 of Pattern D.

From dark blue, cut:
- 32" square for binding.
- 11 (2½"-wide) strips for strip sets.
- 9 (3½"-wide) strips. From these, cut 63 of Pattern D.
- 3 of Pattern E.
- 3 of Pattern E reversed.
- 2 of Pattern F.

From green, cut:
- 16 (2½"-wide) strips for strip sets.
- 8 (3½"-wide) strips. From these, cut 55 of Pattern D.
- 3 of Pattern E.
- 3 of Pattern E reversed.
- 2 of Pattern F.

From light blue, cut:
- 10 (2½"-wide) strips for strip sets.

Strip Sets

Refer to Strip Set Diagrams *throughout.*
1. Make 16 of Strip Set 1, joining green and white strips as shown. Press seams toward green.
2. Place a strip set on cutting mat. Position ruler with 60° marking aligned with bottom edge of strip set (Diagram A). Make first cut to establish a 60° angle.
3. Turn mat to place cut edge to your left. Position ruler with line marking 2½" on cut edge. Cut a 2½"-wide diagonal segment (Diagram B). Cut 13 segments from each Strip Set 1 to get a total of 206 segments. Store segments in zip-top bags until needed for assembly.
4. Make 11 of Strip Set 2, joining dark blue and white strips as shown. Make 9 of Strip Set 3, joining light blue and white strips. Press seam allowances toward blue fabrics.
5. Place 1 of Strip Set 2 on cutting mat. Align ruler's 60° line with bottom edge of strip set as shown (Diagram C). Make first cut to establish 60° angle.
6. Turn strip set or mat to position cut edge to your left. Measuring from cut edge, cut a 6½"-wide diagonal segment (Diagram D). Use 2 rulers, butted together, if neither is wide enough to measure 6½". Cut 5 segments from each Strip Set 2 to get total of 54 segments.

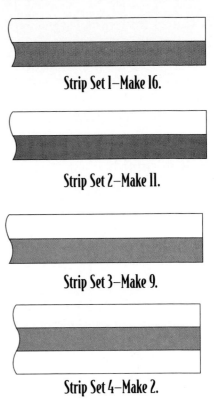

Strip Set 1–Make 16.

Strip Set 2–Make 11.

Strip Set 3–Make 9.

Strip Set 4–Make 2.

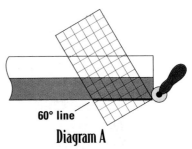

60° line
Diagram A

Diagram B

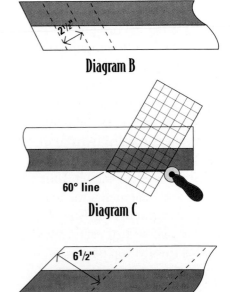

60° line
Diagram C

6½"
Diagram D

continued

7. Cut 41 (6½"-wide) segments from Strip Set 3 in same manner.

8. Use leftover portion of Strip Set 3 and remaining strips to make 2 of Strip Set 4. From these, cut 9 (6½"-wide) segments as before.

Quilt Assembly

Quilt is assembled in diagonal rows, which are joined to form center section of quilt. Refer to **Quilt Assembly Diagram** throughout.

1. For Row 1, select 2 segments of Strip Set 2 and 1 segment of Strip Set 4. Join #2 segments to opposite sides of #4 segment as shown. Make 2 of Row 1. Press all seam allowances toward bottom of row.

2. For Row 2, select 11 Strip Set 1 segments. Join segments, turning every other segment to alternate fabrics as shown. Make 2 of Row 2. Press seam allowances toward top of row.

3. For Row 3, select 4 Strip Set 2 segments, 3 Strip Set 3 segments, and 1 Strip Set 4 segment. For Row 5, select 7 Strip Set 2 segments, 5 Strip Set 3 segments, and 1 Strip Set 4 segment. For Row 7, select 9 segments of Strip Set 2, 8 Strip Set 3 segments, and 1 segment of Strip Set 4. Join units in each row as shown. Make 2 of each row. Press all seam allowances toward bottom of row.

4. For Row 4, join 21 segments of Strip Set 1 as shown. Join 31 Strip Set 1 segments for Row 6 and 40 segments for Row 8 as shown. Make 2 of each row. Press seams toward top of row.

5. For Row 9, select 10 segments of Strip Set 2, 9 segments of Strip Set 3, and 1 segment of Strip Set 4. Join units in a row as shown. Press seam allowances toward bottom of row.

6. Align diagonal rows as shown, matching seams of adjacent units. Join rows in numerical order as shown. Jagged edges will be trimmed when rows are joined.

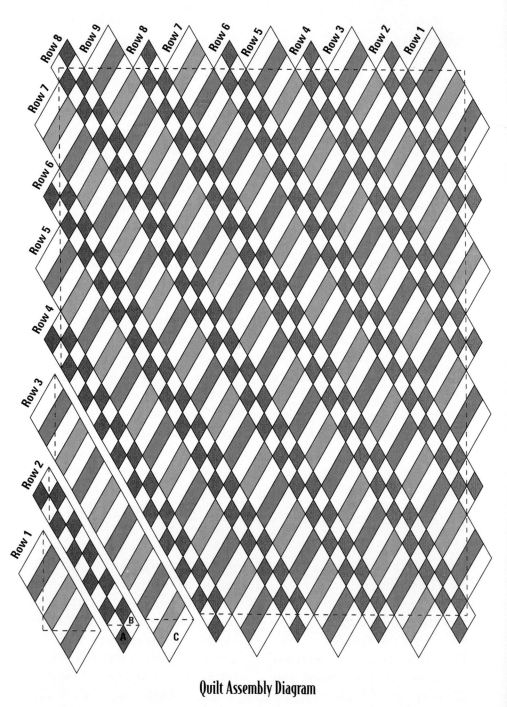

Quilt Assembly Diagram

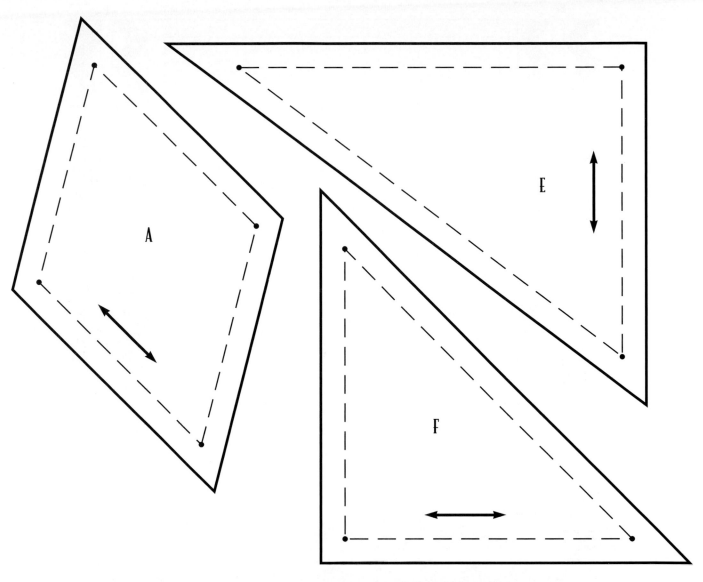

7. Sew 2 scraps of white fabric to light blue strip of each Row 1. Size and shape is unimportant, as these will be trimmed to correct shape when rows are trimmed.
8. To trim edges, use acrylic ruler to measure ¼" below points of green diamonds at each row intersection around edge of quilt (Diagram E). Be sure ruler is correctly aligned to leave seam allowance and that you are cutting a straight edge (outlined in red on assembly diagram). Trim edges on all sides to complete center unit.

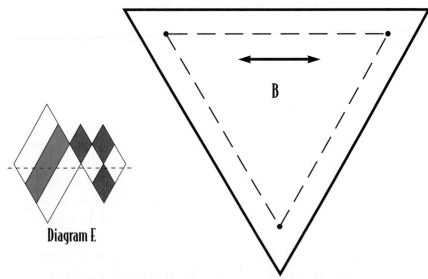

Diagram E

continued

Border Assembly Diagram

Borders

Refer to **Border Assembly Diagram** *throughout.*

1. Measure length of quilt; then trim 3½" x 81" white borders to match quilt length. Sew borders to quilt sides. Press seam allowances toward borders.

2. Measure width of quilt. Trim 3½" x 66" white strips to match quilt width. Sew borders to top and bottom edges of quilt.

3. For left side border, select 20 green D triangles and 20 white Ds. Starting with a green triangle, join 10 green Ds and 10 white Ds in a row. Sew white and green E reversed triangles to row ends as shown. Repeat to make second row of triangles. Turn second row upside down and sew to bottom edge of first row to complete border strip. Sew border to left side of quilt, easing to fit as necessary.

4. Make right border in same manner, adding E triangles to row ends. Sew border to side of quilt.

5. For bottom border, select 15 each of white and green D triangles. Make 2 rows of triangles as shown, ending rows with alternating colors of E and E reversed triangles. Join rows to make bottom border. Then add 2½" x 66" white border to bottom edge.

6. Trim a 3¼" triangle from 1 corner of each G square **(Diagram F)**. Sew green F triangles onto G squares for border corners. Sew corners onto ends of green

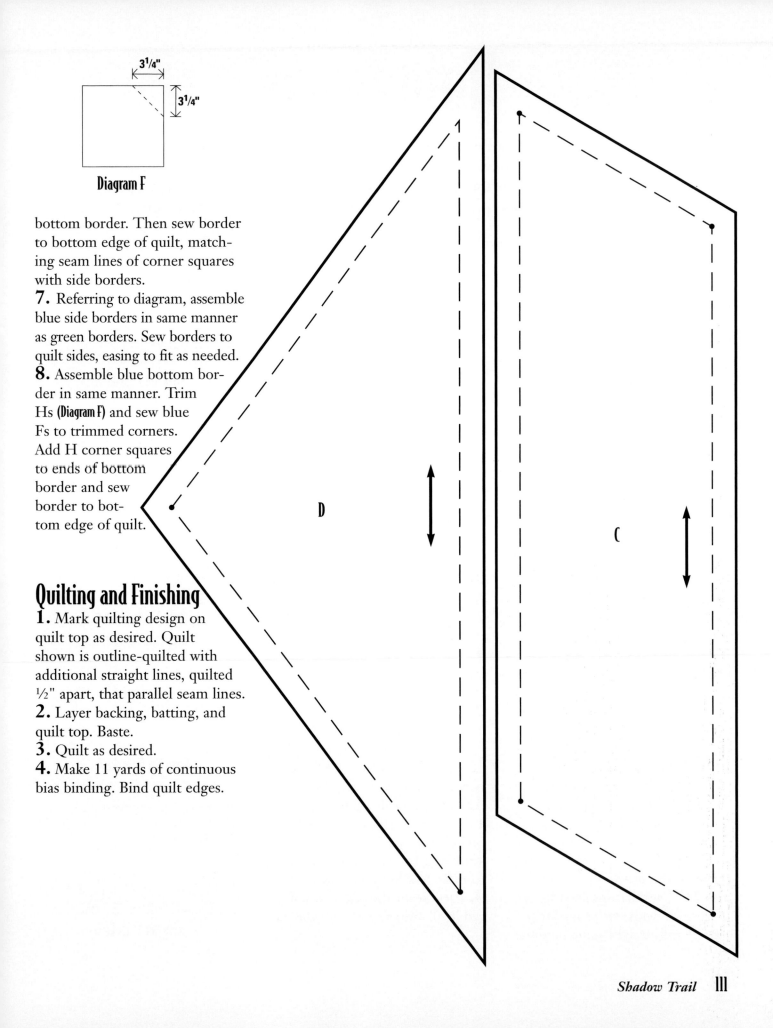

3¼"

3¼"

Diagram F

bottom border. Then sew border to bottom edge of quilt, matching seam lines of corner squares with side borders.

7. Referring to diagram, assemble blue side borders in same manner as green borders. Sew borders to quilt sides, easing to fit as needed.

8. Assemble blue bottom border in same manner. Trim Hs (Diagram F) and sew blue Fs to trimmed corners. Add H corner squares to ends of bottom border and sew border to bottom edge of quilt.

Quilting and Finishing

1. Mark quilting design on quilt top as desired. Quilt shown is outline-quilted with additional straight lines, quilted ½" apart, that parallel seam lines.

2. Layer backing, batting, and quilt top. Baste.

3. Quilt as desired.

4. Make 11 yards of continuous bias binding. Bind quilt edges.

D

C

Homespun

This design of squares and rectangles invites you to try rotary cutting and strip piecing. Start with a solid fabric or a luscious print and then pair it with a coordinating solid. Also known as Burgoyne Surrounded, this quilt looks great in a light-on-dark treatment.

Quilt: 77" x 95"   **Blocks: 20 (15") squares**

Materials

6 yards white or muslin
3 yards red
5⅝ yards backing fabric
90" x 108" precut batting

Cutting

These instructions are for rotary cutting. For traditional piecing, use patterns on page 115.

Strip piecing eliminates the need to cut individual squares and rectangles. Instead, you'll sew strips into sets, which are cut into segments for further piecing. Cut all strips cross-grain, from selvage to selvage. Cut pieces in order listed to make best use of yardage.

From white, cut:
- 34 (1½"-wide) strips for strip sets.
- 8 (2½"-wide) strips for Strip Set 4.
- 25 (3½"-wide) strips. From these, cut 49 (3½" x 15½") sashings.
- 14 (3½"-wide) strips. From these, cut 80 (3½" x 5½") Ds and 160 (2½" x 3½") Bs.

From red, cut:
- 36 (1½"-wide) strips for strip sets.
- 21 (2½"-wide) strips for Strip Set 4 and straight-grain binding.

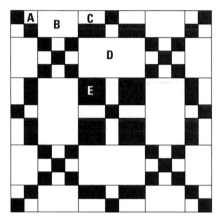

Homespun Block—Make 20.

Strip Sets

See Quilt Smart Workshop, page 156, for tips on rotary cutting. Refer to Strip Set Diagrams *throughout.*

1. Join 1½"-wide white and red strips to make Strip Set 1 as shown. Make 6 of Strip Set 1.

2. For strip sets 2 and 3, join 1½"-wide strips as shown. Make 10 of Strip Set 2 and 6 of Strip Set 3. (These are used for pieced border as well as for blocks.)

3. Use 2½"-wide white strips and 1½"-wide red strips to make 4 of Strip Set 4. Use 2½"-wide red strips and 1½"-wide white strips to make 6 of Strip Set 5 as shown.

4. Press seam allowances toward red in all strip sets.   *continued*

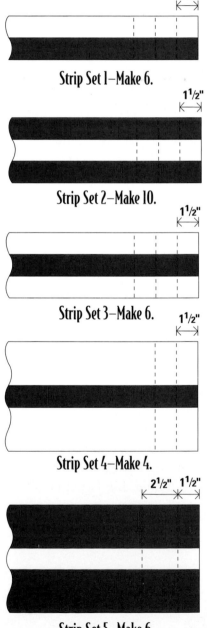

Strip Set 1—Make 6.

Strip Set 2—Make 10.

Strip Set 3—Make 6.

Strip Set 4—Make 4.

Strip Set 5—Make 6.

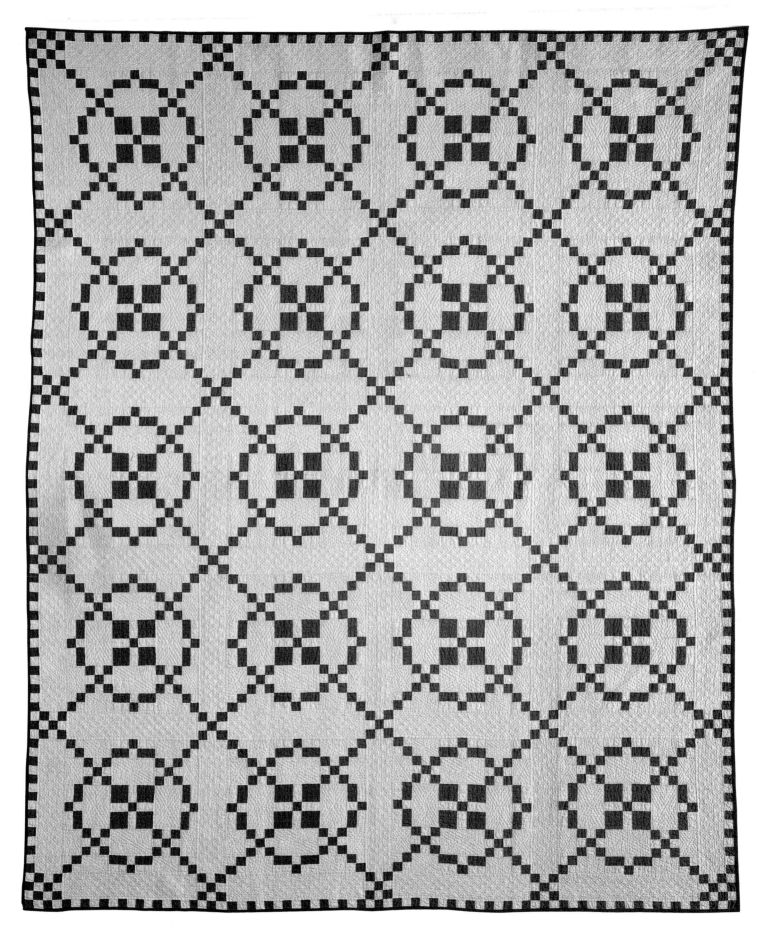

Stars of Alabama

Though no one seems to know why this star is attributed to Alabama, it can't be coincidence that it shines with the colors of Auburn University. Made in 1939 (by a Tigers fan?), this quilt wins cheers for its complementary colors and creative pieced sashing.

Quilt: 71" x 87"   Blocks: 20 (14") squares

Materials

5 yards cream
1¼ yards *each* navy and blue
1 yard *each* orange and peach
2⅛ yards 90"-wide backing fabric
81" x 96" precut batting
Rotary cutter and acrylic ruler
   (optional)

Cutting

These instructions are for rotary cutting. Strip piecing eliminates the need to cut individual diamonds. Instead, you sew strips into sets, which are cut into segments for further piecing. For traditional cutting, use patterns A–E on page 129.

Cut pieces in order listed to make best use of yardage. Cut all strips cross-grain unless otherwise indicated.

From cream, cut:
- 9 (1½"-wide) strips for Strip Set 3.
- 2 (5½" x 93") lengthwise strips and 2 (5½" x 77") lengthwise strips for border.
- 30" square for bias binding.
- 80 (4⅝") B squares. Cut these from fabric left over from border cut.
- 4 (7⅛"-wide) strips. From these, cut 20 (7⅛") squares. Cut each square in quarters diagonally to get 80 C triangles.
- 241 (1¾") E squares.
- 10 (2⅛") squares. Cut each square in quarters diagonally to get 38 D triangles (and 2 extra).

From blue, cut:
- 27 (1½"-wide) strips for strip sets.

From navy, cut:
- 9 (1½"-wide) strips for Strip Set 1.
- 130 (2⅛") squares. Cut each square in quarters diagonally to get 520 D triangles.

From orange and peach, cut:
- 18 (1½"-wide) strips of *each* fabric for strip sets.

Making Strip Sets

Each star is made of 8 identical diamonds or star points. There are 3 rows in each diamond.

1. Start by making a strip set for each row of diamonds. Select a 1½"-wide strip to represent each diamond in that row. For Row 1, select 1 strip each of navy, orange, and blue.

2. Join strips in order (Strip Set 1 Diagram), offsetting ends about 1½" as shown. (It's not necessary for offset to be a precise measurement, as jagged edge is trimmed later. The offset eliminates waste and makes it possible to get more segments from each strip set.) Press seam allowances toward last strip.

3. Assemble 9 of each strip set as shown.

4. Place a strip set on cutting mat. Position ruler over jagged edge of fabric, aligning 45° line on ruler with edge of bottom strip. (You may want to use 2 rulers, butted together, to verify correct alignment.) Rotary-cut along ruler's edge to establish 45° angle (Diagram A).

5. Measuring from cut edge, cut 19 (1½"-wide) segments from each strip set. Cut 160 segments of each type for star diamonds.

continued

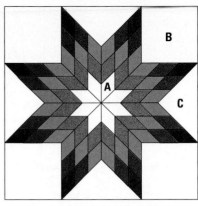

Star of Alabama Block–Make 20.

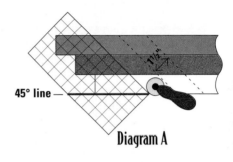

45° line

Diagram A

1½"

Strip Set 1–Make 9.

1½"

Strip Set 2–Make 9.

1½"

Strip Set 3–Make 9.

Making Blocks

1. For each diamond, select 1 segment from each strip set. Arrange segments in order (**Diagram B**). Handle segments carefully to avoid stretching bias edges.

2. With right sides facing, pin Row 2 to Row 1 (**Diagram C**). Insert a pin through each seam of Row 2, ¼" from edge; then push pin through matching seam of Row 1. Pin at ends and middle of rows, too, to hold rows securely together.

3. Sew segments together, using ¼" seam. Stop to remove each pin just before needle can hit it. When seam is complete, check right side. Nicely matched seams are important for a good-looking star, so you may want to resew a seam that doesn't match nicely.

4. Join Row 3 in same manner to complete diamond.

5. Make 8 diamonds for each star.

6. Sew diamonds into pairs, pinning matching seams as before. Sew from center of star (Row 3) to outside edge, stopping ¼" from outside edge (**Diagram D**). Backstitch. Trim excess seam allowance at tips of center diamonds.

7. See page 143 for tips on sewing set-in seams. Sew B squares into openings between each pair (**Block Assembly Diagram**). Press seam allowances toward diamonds.

8. Join 2 diamond pairs to make star half. Then join halves to complete star as shown.

9. Press seam allowances between diamonds in same direction.

10. Set C triangles into openings between diamonds to complete block. Press seam allowances toward diamonds.

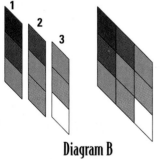

Diagram B

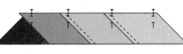

Diagram C

Leave ¼" unsewn.

Diagram D

Block Assembly Diagram

Quilt Assembly

1. For each sashing row, select 7 Es, 2 cream Ds, and 16 navy Ds. Sew navy Ds to opposite sides of each E square **(Sashing Diagram)**. Join cream and navy Ds to make 2 end triangles. Press all seam allowances toward navy. Join units as shown to make 1 sashing row. Make 16 sashing rows.

2. Referring to photo, join blocks and sashing in 4 vertical rows with 5 blocks and 4 sashings in each row.

3. For each vertical sashing row, select 43 Es, 88 navy Ds, and 2 cream Ds. Assemble each row in same manner as short rows, with cream/navy end triangles at each end. Make 3 vertical sashing rows.

4. Join rows as shown.

5. See page 158 for tips on sewing a mitered border. Sew border strips to center section and miter corners.

Quilting and Finishing

1. Mark quilting design on quilt top as desired. Quilt shown is outline-quilted and has cross-hatching (spaced ⅝" apart) in B squares, C triangles, and border.

2. Layer backing, batting, and quilt top. Baste.

3. Outline-quilt patchwork. Add additional quilting as marked or as desired.

4. Make 9 yards of continuous bias binding. Bind quilt edges.

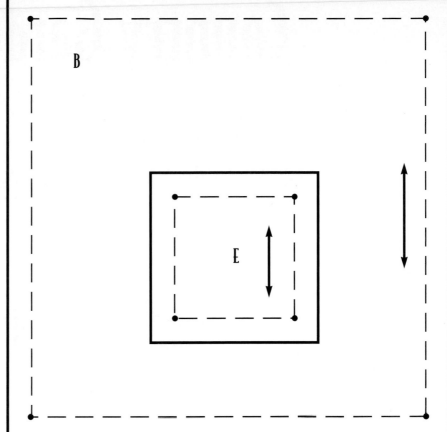

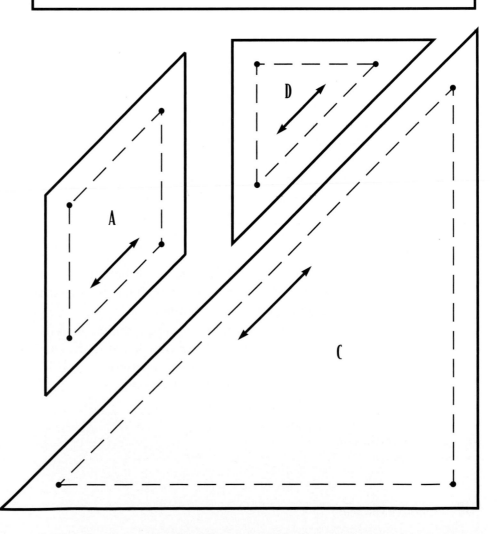

Country Gardens

Stairsteps of stylized flowers create a fantasy garden in this 1941 quilt. Designed by Margaret Hayes of Knoxville, this garden can be planted with blooms of one favorite color or flowers of many colors.

Quilt: 78" x 94"   **Blocks: 50 (8") flower blocks**
49 (8") triangle blocks

Materials
5 yards white or muslin
4¼ yards green
½ yard pink
¼ yard dark pink
5½ yards backing fabric
81" x 96" precut batting
Zip-top plastic storage bags
   (optional)

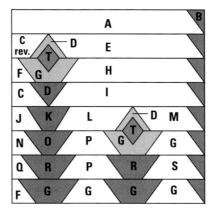

Block 1—Make 50.

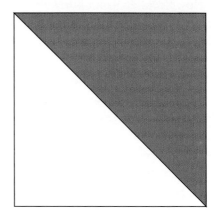

Block 2—Make 49.

Cutting
Make templates of patterns A–S on pages 132, 134 and 135. For appliqué, make template of Pattern T. Add seam allowances when cutting appliqué pieces. Cut pieces in order listed to make best use of yardage. Cut strips cross-grain, from selvage to selvage, unless otherwise indicated.

Several of these pieces are similar in size and shape, so it's easy to get them confused. To keep cut pieces tidy as you sew, we recommend keeping each group in a zip-top plastic bag, labelled with the appropriate letter.

From pink, cut:
• 100 *each* of patterns D and G.

From dark pink, cut:
• 100 of Pattern T.

From white, cut:
• 25 (8⅞") squares for Block 2. *Note:* Remaining pieces can all be cut from 1½"-wide strips.
• 50 *each* of patterns A, C, C reversed, E, H, I, J, L, M, N, Q, and S.
• 100 *each* of patterns F and P.
• 150 of Pattern G.

From green, cut:
• 32" square for binding.
• 4 (3½" x 92") lengthwise strips for borders.
• 25 (8⅞") squares for Block 2.
• 50 *each* of patterns D, K, and O.
• 100 *each* of patterns G and R.
• 400 of Pattern B.

Making Block 1
See Quilt Smart Workshop, page 157, for tips on piecing. Refer to **Block 1 Assembly Diagram** *throughout.*
1. Block 1 is assembled in 8 horizontal rows as shown. Start at block top and work down. For Row 1, join A and B as shown. Press seam allowance toward A.

continued

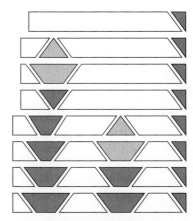

Block 1 Assembly Diagram

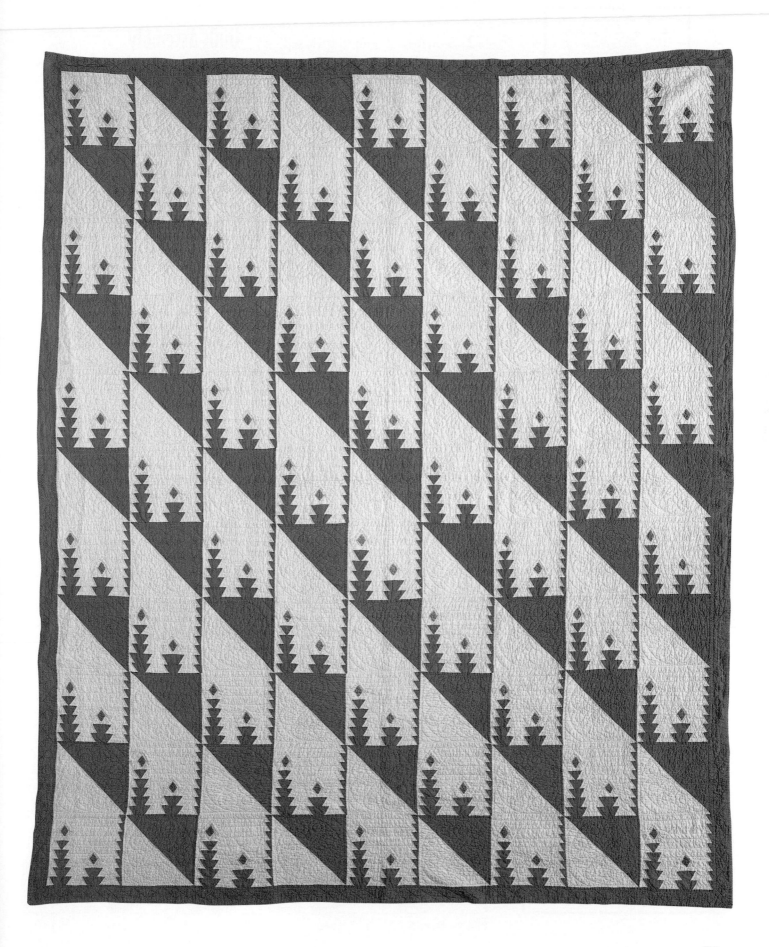

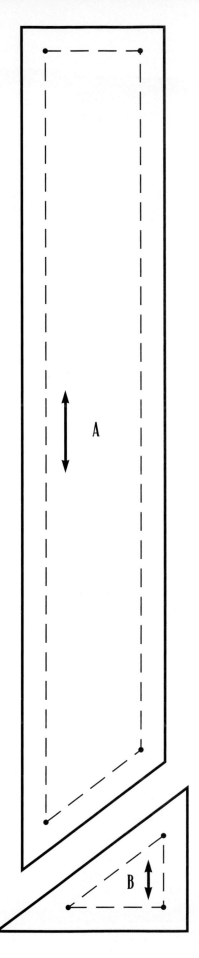

2. For Row 2, join C reversed, pink D, E, and B. *Note:* Press seam allowances toward white pieces throughout block.

3. For Row 3, join F, pink G, H, and B as shown.

4. For Row 4, join C, green D, I, and B.

5. For Row 5, join J, K, L, pink D, M, and B.

6. For Row 6, join N, O, P, pink G, white G, and B.

7. For Row 7, join Q, R, P, R, S, and B.

8. For Row 8, join F, green G, white G, green G, white G, and B.

9. Appliqué T over seam of each D/G flower to complete block.

10. Make 50 of Block 1.

Making Block 2

1. On wrong side of white 8⅞" square, lightly draw a diagonal line from corner to corner.

2. Match white square with green square, right sides facing.

3. Stitch ¼" seam on *both* sides of drawn line (Block 2 Assembly Diagram).

4. Press. Cut on drawn line to get 2 blocks. Press seam allowances toward green.

5. In this manner, make 49 blocks and 1 extra. You can use extra block as a signature patch. (See page 56 for signature patch tips.)

Quilt Assembly

Refer to photo and Row Assembly Diagram *throughout. In row assembly, press seam allowances toward Block 2s.*

1. For Row 1, join 5 of Block 1 and 4 of Block 2. Alternate blocks as shown. Make 6 of Row 1.

2. For Row 2, join 5 of Block 2 and 4 of Block 1 as shown. Make 5 of Row 2.

3. Lay out rows, starting with Row 1 and alternating rows. When satisfied with layout, join rows.

Border

1. Measure length of quilt; then trim 2 border strips to match quilt length. Sew borders to quilt sides. Press seam allowances toward borders.

2. Measure width of quilt; trim remaining border strips to match. Sew borders to top and bottom edges of quilt.

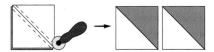

Block 2 Assembly Diagram

Row Assembly Diagram

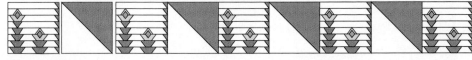

Row 1—Make 6.

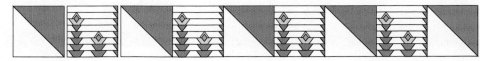

Row 2—Make 5.

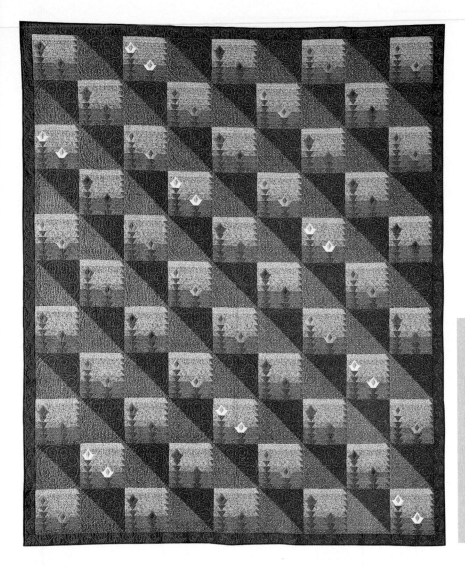

Quilting and Finishing

1. Mark quilting design on quilt top as desired. Quilt shown has outline quilting in Block 1 and a pretty floral wreath (see pattern, page 135) in Block 2.

2. Assemble backing. Layer backing, batting, and quilt top. Baste.

3. Quilt as desired.

4. Make 10 yards of continuous bias binding. Bind quilt edges.

Jennette Maddox of Burnsville, North Carolina, made this bright Country Gardens quilt in 1985, using six colors for her flowers. Jennette's beautiful quilting made this quilt a prizewinner in Mountain Mist's 1985 national contest.

Tying

Tying is a fast and easy way to secure the quilt layers. It's the best way to work with thick batting for puffy comforters. Tying is fine for polyester batting, but not for cotton or silk batts, which require close quilting.

For ties, use pearl cotton, floss, lightweight yarn, or narrow ribbon; these are stable enough to stay tightly tied. You'll also need a sharp needle with an eye large enough to accommodate the tie material.

Thread the needle with 6" of thread or yarn. Do not knot the ends. Starting in the center of your basted quilt top, take a small stitch through all three layers. Center a 3"-long tail on each side of the stitch (Diagram 1). Tie the tails in a tight double knot (Diagram 2).

Make ties up to 4" apart across the surface of the quilt. Trim the tails of all knots to a uniform length.

Bind the quilt as described on page 160. If your quilt has thick batting, you'll want to cut wider binding strips.

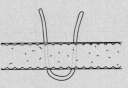

Diagram 1

Diagram 2

C

Q

J

S

E

H

I

L

F

K

T

P

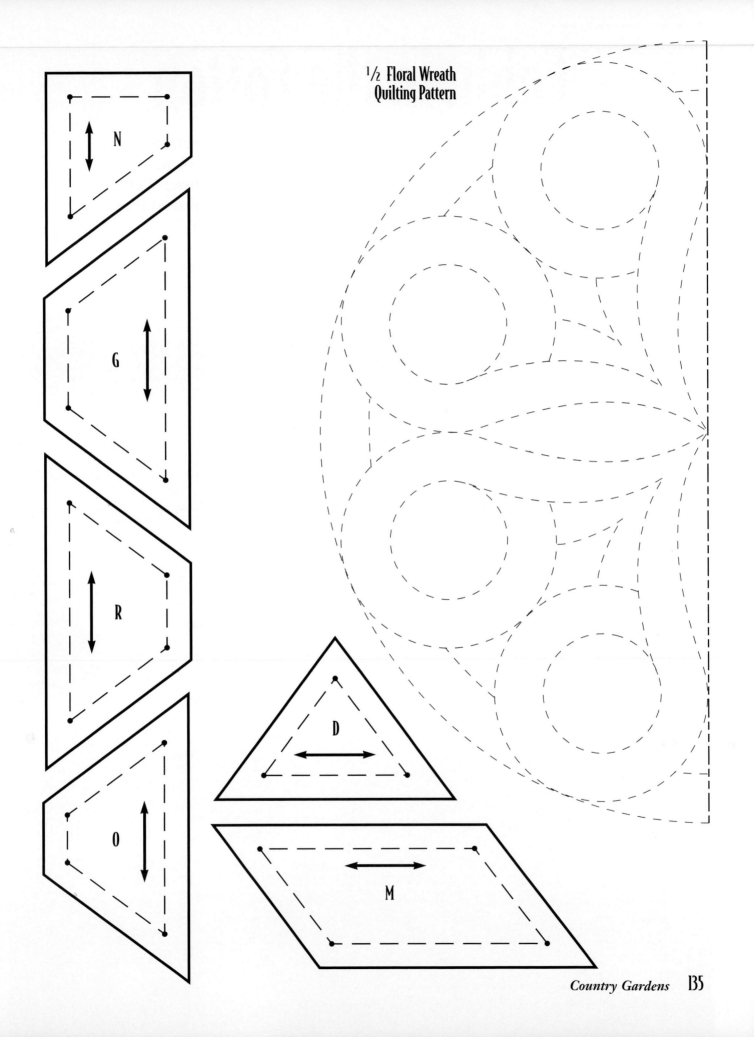

Cabin in the Cotton

This 1930s quilt takes its name from a popular Depression-era novel. The story of sharecroppers battling a greedy plantation owner was made into a film in 1932. The movie features Bette Davis as plantation belle Madge, who utters the immortal line, "I'd like to kiss ya, but I just washed my hair."

Quilt: 78" x 90"   **Blocks: 72 (8¼") squares**
                                          22 (3¾") squares

Materials

3 yards muslin
1 yard lavender
Pastel scraps (approximately
    6½ yards total)
2⅞ yards 90"-wide backing fabric
81" x 96" precut batting
Rotary cutter and acrylic ruler

Cutting

Instructions are for rotary cutting.
For the stitch-and-flip method, it
is not necessary to cut individual
pieces for logs.

From muslin, cut:

- 4 (3" x 90") lengthwise strips
  for outer borders.
- 11 (1¼" x 90") lengthwise strips
  for sashing rows.
- 2 (10¾") squares. Cut squares
  in half diagonally to get 4 triangles for quilt corners.
- 11 (6⅝") squares. Cut squares
  in quarters diagonally to get 44
  triangles for side units.
- 82 (1¼" x 8¾") sashing strips.

From lavender, cut:

- 30" square for bias binding.
- 94 (1¼") squares for block
  centers.

From scrap fabrics, cut:

- 1¼"-wide strips at least 3½"
  long up to 17" long. (You might
  want to start with just a few cut
  strips and cut more as you go.)

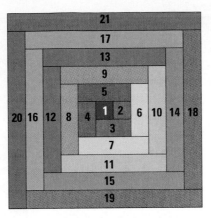

Block 1–Make 72.

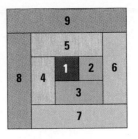

Block 2–Make 22.

Diagram A

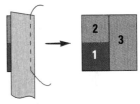

Diagram B

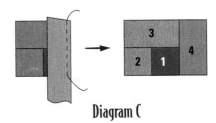

Diagram C

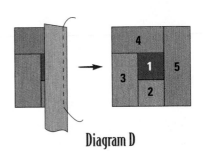

Diagram D

Making Blocks

*See Quilt Smart Workshop, page
157, for tips on piecing.*

1. Start each block with a lavender square.
2. Cut a 1¼" square from first
scrap strip. Join squares (**Diagram A**).
3. For Log 3, match same scrap
to long edge of square pair, right
sides facing; stitch (**Diagram B**). Trim
log even with bottom square.
Press seams toward new log.
4. Turn unit to position new log
at top. With right sides facing,
match another strip to right edge
and stitch (**Diagram C**). Trim Log 4
even with block as before. Press
seam allowance toward new log.
5. Turn unit so newest log is at
top. With right sides facing,
match same strip to right edge of
block and stitch (**Diagram D**). Trim log
even with block and press.
6. Continue adding logs in this
manner until you have 5 logs on
all sides of center square. (See
block diagram for numbered
sequence.) Always press seams
toward newest log. Completed
block will measure 8¾" square.
7. Make 72 of Block 1.
8. Make Block 2 in same manner,
stopping at Log 9. Make 22 of
Block 2.   *continued*

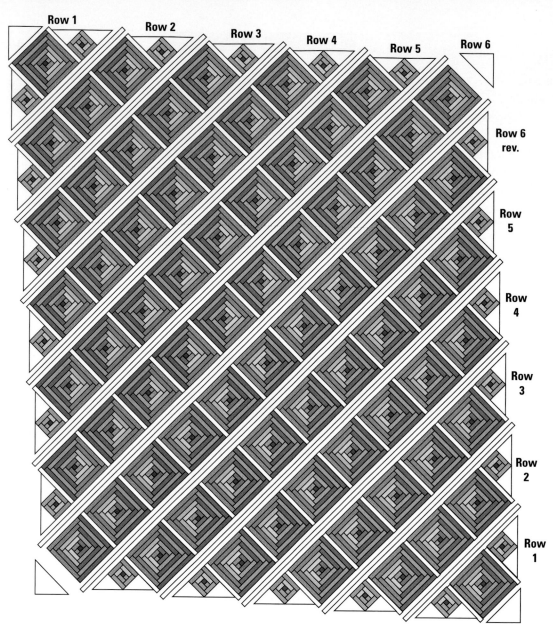

Row 1 Row 2 Row 3 Row 4 Row 5 Row 6

Row 6 rev.

Row 5

Row 4

Row 3

Row 2

Row 1

Quilting Assembly Diagram

Quilt Assembly

Blocks and side units are joined in 12 diagonal rows, with sashing strips between blocks.

1. Sew 2 A triangles to adjacent sides of each Block 2 (Side Unit Diagram). Press seam allowances toward triangles. Make 22 side units.

2. For Row 1, lay out a Block 1, 2 side units, and 2 sashing strips as shown (Quilt Assembly Diagram). Join units in row. Press seam allowances toward sashing strips. Then sew corner triangle to edge of Block 1. Make 2 of Row 1.

3. For Row 2, lay out 3 of Block 1, 2 side units, and 4 sashing strips as shown. Join units in row. Make 2 of Row 2.

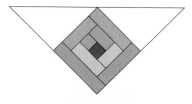

Side Unit–Make 22.

4. Continue to join blocks, sashing strips, and side units in rows as shown. Make 2 each of rows 3, 4, and 5.

5. For Row 6, join 11 blocks, 11 sashing strips, and 1 side unit as shown. Omit corner triangle until quilt assembly is complete. Make 2 of Row 6.

6. Lay out 12 diagonal rows in numerical order as shown. For sashing between rows, measure block rows and cut a strip from

1¼" x 90" muslin strips to fit. Piece 4 longest sashing rows as necessary. Lay out sashing strips between block rows and check placement before joining rows.

7. Join block rows and sashing rows. Trim ends of sashing strips to match ends of block rows.

8. Add corner triangles to ends of each Row 6.

Border

1. Measure length through middle of quilt. Trim 2 borders to match quilt length. Sew borders to quilt sides. Press seam allowances toward borders.

2. Measure width of quilt through middle and trim remaining borders to match quilt width. Sew borders to top and bottom edges of quilt.

Quilting and Finishing

1. Mark quilting design on quilt top as desired. See **Quilting Diagram** for block quilting on quilt shown. A stylish heart (see pattern at right) is quilted in side unit triangles, extending into borders.

2. Layer backing, batting, and quilt top. Baste.

3. Quilt as desired.

4. Make 9⅝ yards of continuous bias binding. Bind quilt edges.

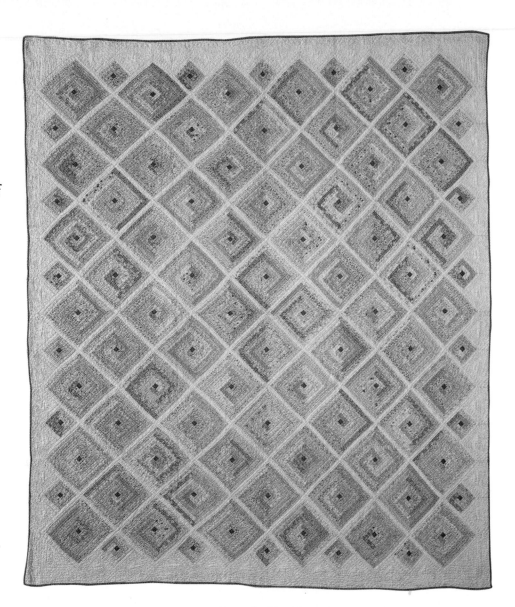

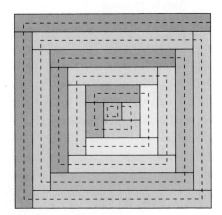

Quilting Diagram

Heart Quilting Pattern

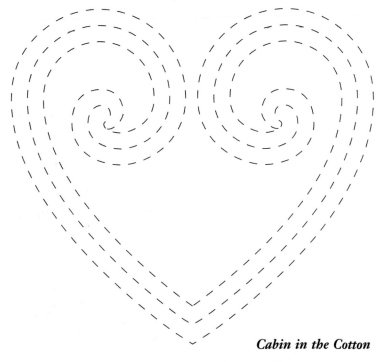

Lone Star

Time has affected some of the fabrics in this 1930s quilt, stitched in the colors of dawn. This kind of deterioration can be caused by chemicals in the dye or by the manner in which the quilt is stored. For tips on how to care for your quilt, see page 145.

Quilt: 79" x 95½"

Materials
4⅝ yards yellow
2 yards lavender
1⅜ yards rose
1 yard pink
1 yard orange
¾ yard blue
¼ yard green
5⅝ yards backing fabric
90" x 108" precut batting
Rotary cutter and 24"-long
   acrylic ruler (optional)

Cutting

Instructions are for rotary cutting. Strip piecing eliminates the need to cut single diamonds. Instead, you sew strips into sets, which are cut into segments for further piecing. For traditional piecing, use Pattern A on page 144.

Cut pieces in order listed to make best use of yardage. Cut cross-grain strips unless otherwise indicated.

From lavender, cut:
• 29 (2¼"-wide) strips. Set aside 9 strips for inner border.

From rose, cut:
• 18 (2¼"-wide) strips. Set aside 9 strips for outer border.

From pink, cut:
• 11 (2¼"-wide) strips. Set aside 9 strips for middle border.

From orange, cut:
• 13 (2¼"-wide) strips.

From blue, cut:
• 10 (2¼"-wide) strips.

From green, cut:
• 3 (2¼"-wide) strips.

From yellow, cut:
• 7 (2¼"-wide) strips for strip sets.
• 2 (8¾" x 72") lengthwise strips for star border.
• 32" square for bias binding.
• 1 (29½") square. Cut this in quarters diagonally to get 4 setting triangles.
• 4 (20½") squares for star corners.

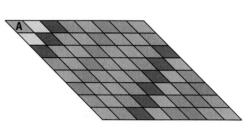

Star Diamond–Make 8.

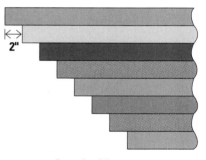

Strip Set 1 Diagram

Making Strip Sets

The Lone Star is made of 8 identical diamonds or star points. There are 8 rows in each diamond.

1. Start by making a strip set for each row of diamond. Select a 2¼"-wide strip to represent each diamond in that row. For Row 1, select 3 lavender strips, 2 orange strips, and 1 strip each of pink, rose, and blue. Arrange strips in order (Strip Set 1 Diagram).

2. Join strips in order as shown, offsetting ends about 2" as shown. (It's not necessary for offset to be a precise measurement, as jagged edge is trimmed later. The offset eliminates waste and makes it possible to get more strips from each strip set.) Press seam allowances toward last strip. *continued*

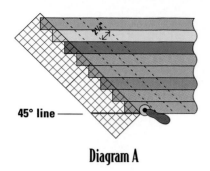

Diagram A

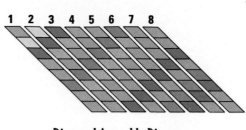

Diamond Assembly Diagram

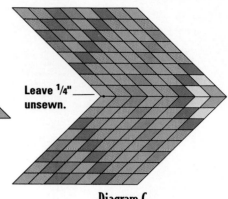

Diagram C

3. Place strip set on cutting mat. Position ruler over jagged edge of fabric, aligning 45° line on ruler with edge of bottom strip. (You may want to use 2 rulers, butted together, to verify alignment along the length of the strip set.) Rotary-cut along edge of ruler to establish 45° angle **(Diagram A)**.

4. Measuring from cut edge, cut 8 (2¼"-wide) segments. Each segment is Row 1 of 1 star diamond.

5. Make strip sets 2–8 in same manner, referring to diagram for color placement. Cut 8 segments from each strip set.

Star Assembly

1. For each diamond, select 1 segment from each strip set. Arrange segments in order **(Diamond Assembly Diagram)**. Handle segments carefully to avoid stretching bias edges.

2. With right sides facing, pin Row 2 to Row 1 **(Diagram B)**. Insert a pin through each seam of Row 2, ¼" from edge; then push pin through matching seam of Row 1. Pin at ends and middle of rows, too, to hold rows securely together.

3. Join segments, using ¼" seam. Stop to remove each pin just before needle can hit it. When

seam is complete, check right side. Nicely matched seams are important for a good-looking star, so you may want to resew a seam that doesn't match nicely.

4. Join remaining rows in same manner to complete star diamond.

5. Sew diamonds into pairs, pinning matching seams as before. Sew from center of star (Row 1) to outside edge, stopping ¼" from outside edge **(Diagram C)**. Backstitch. Trim excess seam allowance at tips of center diamonds.

6. Join 2 pair in same manner to make star half. Then join halves to complete star.

7. Press seam allowances between diamonds in same direction.

8. See page 143 for tips on sewing set-in seams. Sew setting triangles and squares into openings between diamonds (see photo). Press seam allowances toward diamonds.

Borders

1. Measure width of star through center. Trim 2 (8¾"-wide) yellow strips to match quilt width. Sew strips to top and bottom edges of star. Press seam allowances toward borders.

2. For remaining borders, join 2 strips of each color end-to-end to make each top and bottom border. Join 2½ strips to make each side border.

3. Sew lavender and rose strips of same length to opposite sides of each pink border to make combined border for each quilt side.

4. See page 158 for tips on sewing a mitered border. Sew border strips to center section and miter corners.

Quilting and Finishing

1. Mark quilting design on quilt top as desired. Quilt shown has a spoked-wheel design quilted in setting squares (see pattern, page 144). The curved spokes are quilted in a line in star end borders. Remainder of quilt has cross-hatching lines quilted ¼" apart.

2. Assemble backing. Layer backing, batting, and quilt top. Baste.

3. Outline-quilt patchwork. Add additional quilting as marked or as desired.

4. Make 10 yards of continuous bias binding. Bind quilt edges.

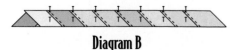

Diagram B

Each generation puts its own stamp on the ever-popular Lone Star. The fabrics in these two quilts are typical of their times. The quilt above radiates with the bright colors of the 1960s. The quilt below was made in 1992 by Barbara Grothaus of Cincinnati, Ohio.

Sewing a Set-in Seam

Setting patchwork pieces into an angled opening requires more than the usual accuracy in sewing. The following steps are helpful in this process.

1. Mark corner dots of seam line on each piece, using a ruler or window template. Use these match points to align pieces when pinning. Join pieces that form an angled opening, sewing from corner dot to corner dot **(Photo A)**. Backstitch at beginning and end of seam, leaving seam allowances open at both ends.

2. To set a piece into the opening, begin by pinning one side of the piece in place, using corner dots as guides **(Photo A)**. Sew pinned seam between dots, starting at outer edge and stopping at corner dot. Backstitch.

3. Realign fabric to pin adjacent side of set-in piece to opposite side of opening, right sides facing **(Photo B)**. Start each seam at inside corner dot. Stitch and backstitch, making sure stitches don't pass dot and go into seam allowance. Stitch to outside edge. Press seam allowances open or to 1 side, as you prefer.

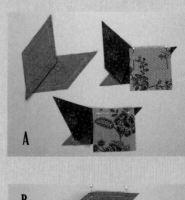

A

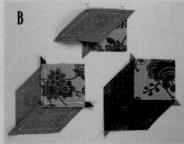

B

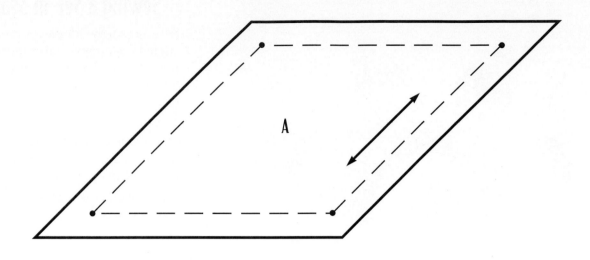

A

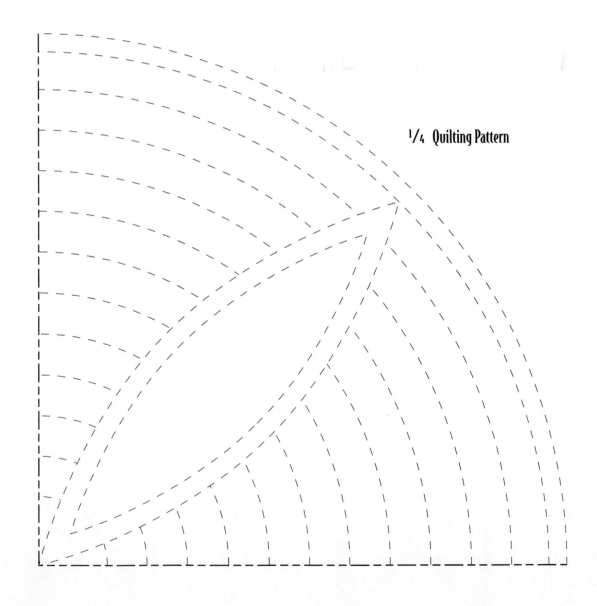

¼ Quilting Pattern

Care and Cleaning

We all want to display the quilts we love. But we must remember to protect them from harmful elements so they will last to warm generations to come.

Shield quilts from direct light and heat, dust, damp, smoke, and aerosol sprays. The following tips for display, storage, and cleaning are suitable for most quilts. A museum-quality heirloom has special needs; if you have one, get expert advice on its care.

Washing Up

Any quilt that is used will eventually need to be cleaned. You can wash a quilt if fabrics were prewashed and tested for colorfastness before the quilt was made. When in doubt, test a corner of a finished quilt to be sure dyes do not bleed. (If fabrics bleed, your only choice may be dry cleaning.)

Some people trust today's fabrics enough to toss a quilt in a large-capacity washing machine. Others prefer to wash a quilt by hand in a tub. Follow these tips to wash your quilt safely.

• Use a mild soap in cold water. Never use bleach. Many experts suggest Mountain Mist® Ensure® Quilt Wash, a soap designed to gently dissolve and rinse soil with little or no agitation. Free of chemicals found in detergents, Ensure cleans a quilt nicely. It is available at quilt and fabric shops, and from mail-order sources.

• The heat and agitation of a dryer takes the life out of fabric, so air drying is best. Dry a wet quilt by laying it flat on the floor or outside in the shade. Place clean towels on the grass and lay the quilt on the towels. A wet quilt is heavy, so be sure to gently squeeze out excess water; then lift and carry the quilt in a way that avoids putting stress on the seams.

• Avoid dry cleaning if possible. The chemicals in cleaning fluids can be harmful. However, if you've determined that the quilt's fabrics may bleed, this may be the only way to remove stains.

Tucked Away

When not in use, store your quilts in a cool, dry place, each in its own acid-free wrapping. Winter cold and summer heat make attics and garages inappropriate storage areas. Basements are off-limits, too, if there is the slightest risk of dampness.

Do not store quilts in plastic, which traps moisture and encourages growth of mildew. Instead, put each quilt in a cotton pillowcase or wrap it in acid-free tissue paper (available from mail-order catalogs, see page 73). Boxes made of acid-free material are also available. Crumpled acid-free paper placed inside each fold prevents creases from developing along fold lines. These materials let air circulate but still protect the quilt from dust and damp.

If you keep your quilt on a rack or in a chest, put a few layers of acid-free paper or muslin between the quilt and the wood. The natural acids in wood will eventually stain the cloth.

Each time you put a quilt away, fold it differently to prevent damage where fabric fibers become cracked and weak. If possible, avoid folds altogether by rolling the quilt around a tube or cotton towel.

Fading

Exposure to light takes a toll on fabric, so all quilts fade to some degree over time. Some fabrics fade faster and more drastically than others, and there is no sure way to identify these fabrics beforehand. However, here is a simple test that is worthwhile if you have time.

Before you make your quilt, cut a 4" square of each prewashed fabric and tape the squares to a sunny window. A month later, compare the squares with the remaining yardage. If the squares are faded to the same degree, you can assume the finished quilt will keep a uniform appearance as it ages. But if one fabric fades more than the others, you might want to select another for your quilt.

A Breath of Air

By changing the quilt on your bed often, no one quilt is exposed for long. Rotate quilts with the change of seasons, for their own good as well as for a fresh look.

All quilts collect dust. Before you put a quilt away for the season, shake it and air it outdoors. A breezy, overcast day is best if the humidity is low. Lay towels on the grass or over a railing; then spread the quilt over the towels. Keep the quilt out of direct sunlight.

Snowbound

The starry flake featured in Whittier's lovely poem (excerpted at right) is represented here in cool blue fabrics that make a cozy quilt for frosty nights. With a little practice, the set-in seams of these blocks are fun to sew. (See *Sewing a Set-in Seam*, page 143.)

Quilt: 81" x 94"   Blocks: 99 (6") squares

Materials

4¼ yards white or muslin
3¼ yards dark blue
1⅝ yards light blue
2¾ yards 90"-wide backing fabric
90" x 108" precut batting

Cutting

Make templates of patterns A–E on pages 149 and 150. Cut pieces in order listed to make best use of yardage.

From white, cut:
- 2 (6" x 99") and 2 (6" x 86") lengthwise strips for outer border.
- 2 (5½" x 82") and 2 (5¼" x 70") lengthwise strips for middle border. Because difference in width is so slight, mark which is which to avoid confusion later.
- 20 (1¾"-wide) cross-grain strips. From these, cut 400 of Pattern A.
- 4 (2⅛"-wide) cross-grain strips. From these, cut 49 of Pattern E.
- 216 (2¼") C squares.

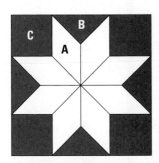

Block 1–Make 50.

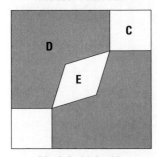

Block 2–Make 49.

From dark blue, cut:
- 32" square for binding.
- 8 (1½"-wide) cross-grain strips for inner border.
- 11 (3¾"-wide) cross-grain strips. From these, cut 111 (3¾") squares. Cut each square in quarters diagonally to get 444 B triangles.
- 11 (2¼"-wide) cross-grain strips. From these, cut 200 (2¼") C squares.

From light blue, cut:
- 98 of Pattern D.

Making Block 1

See page 143 for tips on sewing set-in seams.

1. Join 4 pairs of A diamonds as shown **(Block 1 Assembly Diagram)**. Press joining seam allowances open.
2. Set a C square into opening of each pair.
3. Join 2 diamond pairs. Set a B triangle into each new opening.
4. Join halves. Press seam allowance open.
5. Set B triangles into new openings to complete block.
6. Make 50 of Block 1.

Making Block 2

1. Select 2 D pieces for each block. Sew a C square onto 1 end of each D **(Block 2 Assembly Diagram)**. Press seam allowances toward Cs.
2. Set an E diamond into 1 D; then set diamond into second D piece. Press seam allowances toward Ds.
3. Stitch free edge of each C square to opposite D piece to complete block.
4. Make 49 of Block 2.

continued

Block 1 Assembly Diagram

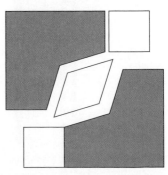

Block 2 Assembly Diagram

Row Assembly Diagram

Row 1—Make 6.

Row 2—Make 5.

Diagram A

Quilt Assembly

1. Quilt is assembled in 11 horizontal rows. For each Row 1, lay out 5 of Block 1 and 4 of Block 2 (Row Assembly Diagram). Lay out 6 of Row 1.

2. For Row 2, lay out 5 of Block 2 and 4 of Block 1. Lay out 5 of Row 2.

3. When satisfied with layout, join blocks in each row. Press seam allowances toward Block 2s.

4. Referring to photo and Quilt Assembly Diagram, join rows, alternating rows 1 and 2 as shown.

Quilt Assembly Diagram

Borders

See page 158 for tips on sewing a mitered border.

1. Join 2 dark blue border strips end-to-end for each inner border. Matching centers, sew a blue strip to 1 long edge of each white middle border strip.

2. Place borders with wider white strips at top and bottom edges and narrower strips at quilt sides. Match centers and raw edges of blue strips to edge of quilt, right sides facing. Stitch borders to center section and miter corners.

3. For each side border, join 2 B triangles to each of 31 C squares **(Diagram A)**. Press seam allowances toward squares. Join units to make side border. At ends of each border, add an extra triangle as shown.

4. Sew side borders to quilt, easing to fit as necessary. Trim end triangles even with edge of quilt.

5. Join B triangles to 28 squares each for top and bottom borders in same manner. Add extra triangles at row ends.

6. Sew border strips to top and bottom edges of quilt, easing to fit. Trim end triangles even with edge of quilt.

7. Sew outer border strips to quilt and miter corners.

Quilting and Finishing

1. Mark quilting design on quilt top as desired. Quilt shown is outline-quilted, with a leaf pattern (page 150) scattered in borders.

2. Layer backing, batting, and quilt top. Baste.

3. Quilt as marked or as desired.

4. Make 10 yards of continuous bias binding. Bind quilt edges.

D

Leaf
Quilting
Pattern

A

E

B

C

Repeat pattern here.

Repeat pattern here.

Guide Post

Pick two tones of a favorite color, and you have the ingredients for this bold, geometric quilt. In solids or prints, the design's strong lines point the way to a quilt that's pure pleasure to make and to see.

Quilt: 84" x 102"

Materials
4 yards gold
3½ yards yellow
3 yards white or muslin
3 yards 90"-wide backing fabric
90" x 108" precut batting

Cutting

Instructions are for rotary cutting and/or traditional cutting. For traditional methods, make templates from patterns on page 155.

Strip-piecing eliminates the need to cut individual diamonds and stripes. Instead, you sew strips into sets, which are cut into segments for further piecing. Cut all strips cross-grain unless otherwise indicated.

From gold, cut:
- 36 (2½"-wide) strips for strip sets.
- 9 (1½"-wide) strips for inner border.
- 32" square for bias binding.
- 4 (2½" x 32") strips (waste from binding square). From these, cut 16 of Pattern A and 10 of Pattern E.

From yellow, cut:
- 36 (2½"-wide) strips for strip sets.
- 9 (2½"-wide) strips for middle border.
- 2 (3⅛"-wide) strips. From these, cut 34 of Pattern D and 4 of Pattern A.

From white, cut:
- 4 (3½" x 100") lengthwise strips for outer borders.
- 14 (4½" x 29") strips. From these, cut 77 of Pattern B.
- 2 (5⅜" x 29") strips. From these, cut 16 of Pattern C.

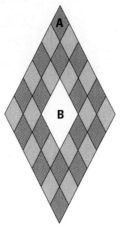

Guide Post Block-Make 16.

Strip Sets

1. Join gold and yellow strips (Diagram A). Make 36 strip sets. Press seam allowances toward gold.
2. Place a strip set on cutting mat. Position ruler with 60° marking aligned with bottom edge of strip set as shown (Diagram A). Make first cut to remove selvage and establish a 60° angle.

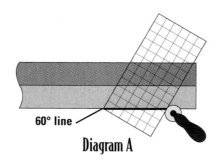

60° line

Diagram A

2½"

Diagram B

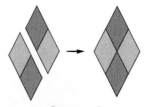

Diagram C

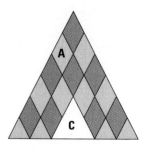

Half-Block–Make 8.

3. Turn strip set or mat to position cut edge to your left. Place ruler with line marking 2½" on cut edge; then cut a 2½"-wide diagonal segment (Diagram B). Cut 13 segments from each strip set to get total of 464 segments.
4. Join 2 segments to make each diamond (Diagram C). Make 232 (128 for blocks, 24 for half-blocks, 74 for sashing units, and 6 for side and corner units).

Making Blocks

See Quilt Smart Workshop, page 157, for tips on piecing.
1. Each block has 8 diamonds and 1 B diamond. Join 3 diamonds in a row for first and third rows of block (Block Assembly Diagram). Press seam allowances away from center.

Block Assembly Diagram

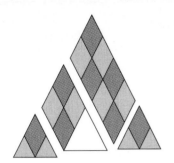

Half-Block Assembly Diagram

2. For middle row, join 2 diamonds to B. Press seam allowances toward B.

3. Join rows to complete block. Make 16 blocks.

4. For half-blocks, join 2 Ds to a gold A. Make 16 A/D units. Press seam allowances toward A.

5. Each half-block has 3 diamonds, 1 C, and 2 A/D units. Join units in rows as shown (**Half-Block Assembly Diagram**); then join rows to complete half-block. Make 8 half-blocks.

Sashing, Side & Corner Units

1. For Sashing Unit 1, join 2 diamonds and 1 B as shown. Press seam allowances toward B. Make 18 of Sashing Unit 1.

2. Sashing Unit 2 is a mirror image of Unit 1. Be sure to sew diamonds onto opposite sides of B as shown. Make 17 of Sashing Unit 2.

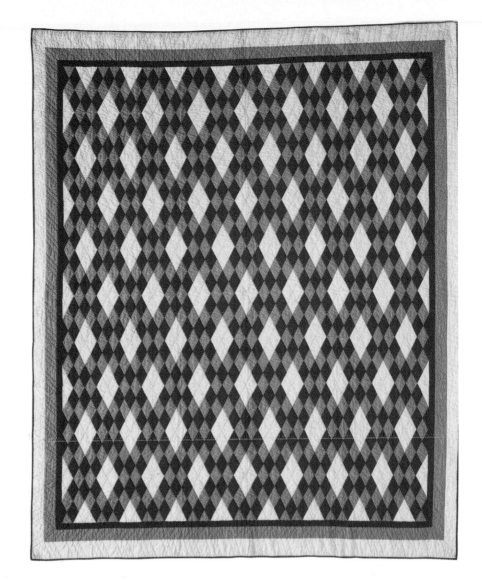

3. For Sashing Unit 3, sew a B to opposite sides of 1 diamond as shown. Make 4 of Sashing Unit 3.

4. For Side Unit, join 2 Es to adjacent sides of each yellow A.

Press seam allowances toward Es. Sew 1 A/E unit and 1 B to adjacent sides of a diamond to make each Side Unit as shown. Make 4 Side Units. *continued*

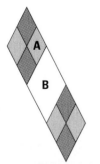

Sashing Unit 1—Make 18.

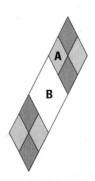

Sashing Unit 2—Make 17.

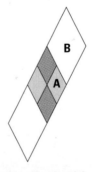

Sashing Unit 3—Make 4.

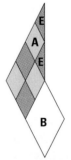

Side Unit—Make 4.

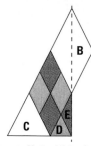

Corner Unit–Make 2.

5. For Corner Unit, join E and D triangles. Sew E/D unit to side of diamond. Sew C and B to opposite sides of diamond as shown. Press seam allowances toward C and B. Make 2 Corner Units.

6. On each corner unit, align ruler with seam line of D/E. Trim excess fabric from Bs.

Quilt Assembly

Quilt is assembled in diagonal rows, alternating blocks and sashing units. Refer to **Quilt Assembly Diagram** throughout, starting at bottom right corner of diagram.

1. For Row 1, select 1 block, 1 half-block, 1 Side Unit, 1 of Sashing Unit 1, and 1 Corner Unit. Sew half-block, sashing unit, block, and side unit in a diagonal row as shown. Sew Corner Unit to sashing/block edge. Make 2 of Row 1. Align ruler with corner unit to trim excess fabric from block and side unit.

2. Lay out remaining blocks, half-blocks, Sashing Unit 1s, and side units in diagonal rows as shown. There are 2 each of rows 2 and 3. (Like Row 1, Row 2 at left is upside down from Row 2 at right. Row 3s are the same.) Join units in each row.

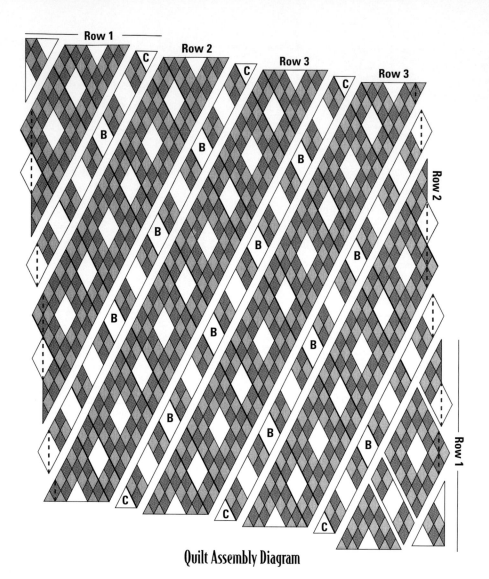

Quilt Assembly Diagram

3. Lay out joined rows as shown. Then lay out remaining sashing units to make 5 diagonal rows between block rows. Fill in between sashing units with B diamonds and end rows with C triangles as shown. When satisfied with position, join units in each row.

4. Lay out block rows and sashing rows again, checking them against diagram to verify correct placement of units. When satisfied with rows, join rows in order as shown.

5. Align ruler with straight edges to trim Bs around edges. Trim Row 3 corners in same manner.

Borders

1. Join 2½ gold border strips end-to-end for each side border. Join 2 borders end-to-end for each top and bottom border.

2. Measure length through middle of quilt; then trim side borders to match quilt length. Sew borders to quilt sides. Press seam allowances toward borders.

3. Measure width through middle of quilt. Trim top and bottom borders to match width. Sew borders to top and bottom edges of quilt.

4. Repeat steps 1–3 for yellow middle border. Repeat steps 2 and 3 for white outer border.

Quilting and Finishing

1. Mark quilting design on quilt top as desired. Quilt shown is outline-quilted with straight bisecting B diamonds.

2. Layer backing, batting, and quilt top. Baste.

3. Quilt as desired.

4. Make 10⅝ yards of continuous bias binding. Bind quilt edges.

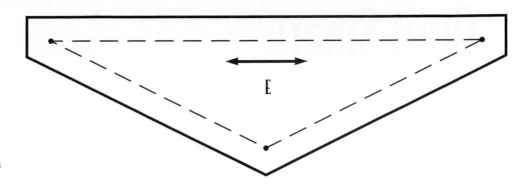

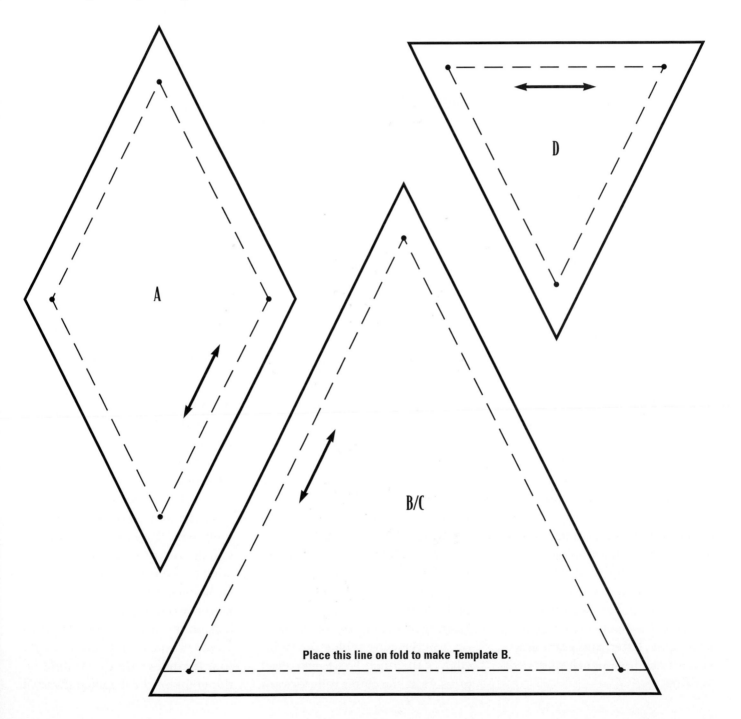

Place this line on fold to make Template B.

Quilt Smart Workshop

A Guide to Quiltmaking

This is an introduction to basic quiltmaking methods. For more comprehensive instructions, we recommend *Quilter's Complete Guide*, published by Oxmoor House. See page 2 of this book for ordering information.

Preparing Fabric

Use 100% cotton fabric. Wash, dry, and press fabrics. Trim selvages before you cut the fabric.

Cutting with Templates

In traditional quiltmaking, a quilter makes a template of the printed pattern. Our grandmothers used cardboard or sandpaper, but we prefer template plastic, available at craft and quilt shops.

1. Place the transparent plastic on the printed page. Trace the pattern as accurately as possible, using a permanent fine-tip marker. For machine piecing, trace the outside solid (cutting) line. For hand piecing, trace the inside broken (sewing) line. Only one line is given for appliqué.

2. Cut out template on drawn line. Place template over printed pattern to compare for accuracy.

3. Label the template with pattern name, letter, and grain line. Use a small hole punch to cut corner dots.

4. Place the template facedown on the wrong side of the fabric and mark around the shape with a sharp pencil. If you are piecing by machine, pencil lines represent cutting lines. For hand piecing, the pencil lines are seam lines, so you must leave about ¾" between marked lines for seam allowances; add ¼" seam allowance around each piece as you cut.

5. Mark match points (corner dots) on each piece.

Rotary Cutting

A rotary cutter, used with a cutting mat and an acrylic ruler, enables you to cut pieces faster and more accurately than with templates. This isn't the traditional method, but our grandmothers knew a good thing when they met one and so do we. Rotary cutting makes possible a number of strip-cutting and quick-piecing techniques. If this tool is new to you, take the time to master its use.

The first step in accurate rotary cutting is to straighten the raw edges of the fabric. This ensures that the pieces you cut will be true.

1. Fold the fabric in half; then fold it in half again. Place the fabric on the mat with excess yardage to your left. (Left-handers should reverse directions.)

2. Align the fold with one horizontal grid line on the mat. Align your ruler with one of the vertical grid lines, just to the left of the raw edge of the fabric (Diagram 1).

3. Hold the ruler firmly in place. Starting at the bottom of the fabric, roll the cutter along the right edge of the ruler. Exert firm, even pressure as the cutter rolls forward.

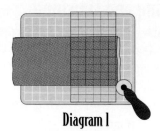

Diagram 1

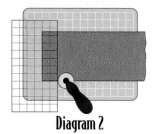

Diagram 2

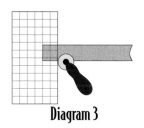

Diagram 3

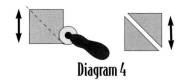

Diagram 4

Diagram 5

4. To cut strips, turn the fabric (or the mat) around so the clean cut is on the left. Align the desired ruler measurement with the trimmed edge of the fabric and cut (Diagram 2).

5. To cut squares and rectangles, align the desired ruler measurement with the end of the strip. Cut across the strip on the right edge of the ruler (Diagram 3).

6. Cut a square in half diagonally to get two triangles with short legs on the straight-grain (Diagram 4).

7. Cut a square in quarters to get four triangles with the straight of the grain on the diagonal (Diagram 5).

To do this, make the first diagonal cut and then rotate the mat (don't lift the fabric) so you can align the ruler on the opposite diagonal and cut again. These triangles are often used for setting pieces in a diagonal-set quilt.

Hand Piecing

Quilts made in the days before sewing machines were sewn entirely by hand. Many people still enjoy hand piecing, especially if they want a portable project.

1. Place two pieces together, right sides facing. Insert a pin through the match points of both pieces **(Diagram 6)**. Adjust pieces as needed to align match points. (Raw edges of the two pieces may not be exactly aligned.)

2. Pin pieces securely together.

3. With a small running stitch, sew from match point to match point. Check to be sure you are stitching in the seam line of both pieces. Begin and end stitching at match points; do not stitch into the seam allowances.

4. When joining units where seams come together, do not sew over seam allowances; sew through them where seam lines meet **(Diagram 7)**.

5. Press both seam allowances to one side. Pressing a seam open, as in dressmaking, may leave gaps between the stitches through which batting fibers can migrate. Press seam allowances toward the darker fabric whenever possible.

6. When four or more seams meet, such as at the corner of a block, press seam allowances in a "swirl" to reduce bulk **(Diagram 8)**.

Machine Piecing

Machine sewing is fast and accurate. In addition to these basic methods, most quick-piecing techniques are designed for machine piecing and rotary cutting.

1. Place two fabric pieces with right sides facing. Align match points as described under Hand Piecing and pin securely.

2. Use a presser foot that gives a ¼" seam allowance, or measure ¼" from the needle and mark that point on the throat plate. Do not backstitch to lock seams. Sew 12 to 15 stitches per inch.

3. Chain-piece units, stitching from edge to edge, to save time when sewing similar pieces **(Diagram 9)**. Join the first unit as usual. At the end of the seam, do not cut the thread or lift the presser foot. Instead, feed in the next unit and continue sewing. Keep stitching until all the units are sewn. Carry the chain to the ironing board and cut units apart as you press.

4. Press seam allowances toward the darker fabric whenever possible. When you join blocks or rows, press the top row in one direction and the next row in the opposite direction to offset seam allowances **(Diagram 10)**.

Hand Appliqué

Hand appliqué is the best way to achieve the antique look of Mountain Mist quilts. We recommend freezer paper (sold in grocery stores) because it eliminates the need to baste seam allowances.

1. Make templates without seam allowances.

2. Trace a template onto the dull side of the freezer paper; then cut

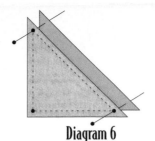

Diagram 6

Diagram 7

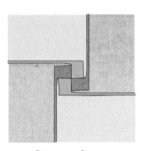

Diagram 8

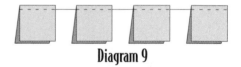

Diagram 9

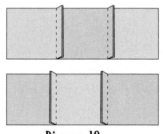

Diagram 10

out the paper shape on the drawn line. Make a freezer-paper shape for every piece to be appliquéd.

3. Pin paper shape, shiny side up, to the wrong side of the appliqué fabric. Following the paper edge, add ¼" seam allowance as you cut the piece. Do not remove pins.

continued

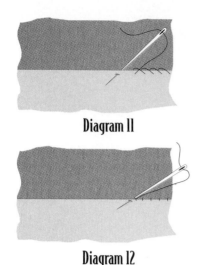

Diagram 11

Diagram 12

4. Use the tip of a hot, dry iron to press seam allowances onto the freezer paper. The softened wax makes the fabric stick. Be careful not to touch the freezer paper with the iron. Do not press seam allowances that will be covered by another piece. Remove pins.
5. Pin each appliqué in place on the background fabric.
6. Use a tiny slipstitch (Diagram 11) or blindstitch (Diagram 12) to appliqué the shape to the background. Use one strand of sewing thread in a color to match the appliqué.
7. When stitching is done, cut away background fabric behind the appliqué, leaving ¼" seam allowance. Separate freezer paper from the fabric with your fingernail and pull gently to remove it.

Borders

It's important to measure your quilt for borders. Measure *through the center*, not along the edges, because the sides may be unequal.

Straight-Sewn Corners
1. Measure quilt length through the middle from top to bottom

(Diagram 13). Trim two border strips to that measurement. Sew strips to quilt sides, easing as needed.
2. Measure across the width of the quilt, including side borders and seam allowances (Diagram 14). Cut borders to this length and sew them to top and bottom edges of the quilt, easing as necessary (Diagram 15).
3. To add more borders, repeat steps 1 and 2 as needed. By making the quilt fit measured strips, the finished quilt will be square and ripple-free.

Mitered Corners
When sewing multiple borders that will be mitered, sew strips together to create one striped unit for each side of the quilt. This makes it easier to match fabrics at the corners.
1. On the wrong side of the quilt top, make a pencil mark exactly ¼" from each corner. Use a pin to mark the center of each side.
2. Determine the length of the quilt, measuring through the middle (Diagram 16).
3. Mark center of each side border strip with a pin. Center the quilt's lengthwise measurement on the border strip, making pencil marks at each side of center to mark corner points as shown.
4. Place border on quilt side, matching right sides and raw edges. Match centers; then insert pins through both layers to align corner match points. Pin the rest of the border to quilt as needed.
5. Sew the border to the quilt using a ¼" seam, starting and ending at marked corner points (Diagram 17). Backstitch at both ends.
6. Add remaining borders in same manner.

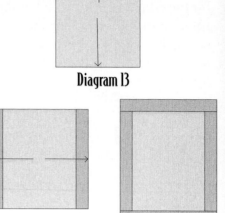

Diagram 13

Diagram 14

Diagram 15

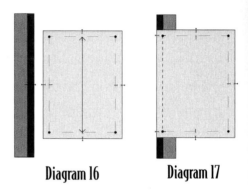

Diagram 16

Diagram 17

Diagram 18

7. With right sides facing, fold the quilt in half diagonally at one corner to align adjacent borders (Diagram 18). Pin.
8. Align the 45°-angle guideline of an acrylic ruler with the long raw edge of the border strip and the edge of the ruler with the fold (Diagram 19). Draw a line along the ruler's edge as shown, from match point to the edge of the border strip. Pin along drawn line.

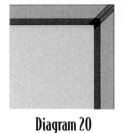

Diagram 19

Diagram 20

Diagram 21

9. Beginning with a backstitch at the inside corner, stitch on the marked line to the outside edge. Check the right side of the quilt to see that the seam lies flat and stripes match as desired.
10. Trim excess fabric to a ¼" seam allowance. Press mitered seam open or to one side, as you prefer (Diagram 20).

Marking the Quilt Top

When the quilt top is complete, it should be pressed and then marked with quilting designs. Use a stencil, purchased or homemade, and mark the design with a silver quilter's pencil. Use a white chalk pencil on dark fabrics. Lightly mark the quilt top with your chosen quilting designs.

Straight outline quilting or cross-hatching can be marked with masking tape as you quilt.

Making a Backing

Backing should be the same type of fabric used for the top. Prewash backing and trim selvages.

This book gives yardage for the width of backing fabric that is most practical for the specific quilt. In some cases, one length of 90"-wide or 108"-wide fabric is specified to avoid waste. When

yardage is given for 45"-wide fabric, the fabric must be cut and pieced to fit the quilt.

A three-panel backing wears better and lies flatter than a two-panel type. It avoids a center seam, which can make a ridge down the middle where the quilt is usually folded. Follow these directions to piece backing.
1. Cut the yardage in half to get two equal lengths of fabric.
2. Cut one length of fabric in half lengthwise to get two panels.
3. Sew a narrow panel to each side of the wide piece (Diagram 21). Press seam allowances open.

Layering and Basting

Place the backing on a flat surface, right side down. Lay the batting on top of the backing, smoothing out wrinkles. Lay the quilt top right side up on the batting. Be sure all edges are aligned.

Use a darning needle and sewing thread for basting. Begin in the center and baste toward the edges. Stitches should cover an ample amount of the quilt so that the layers do not shift during quilting. Inadequate basting can result in puckers and folds on the back and front of the quilt.

You can use safety pins for basting instead of needle and thread.

Quilting

You can quilt by machine or by hand. Machine quilting is a technique that requires more explanation than is possible here. For information on machine quilting, see *Quilter's Complete Guide*.

Hand quilting is done with the quilt in a hoop or in a frame. Use a needle called a between, available in sizes 7 (the longest) to 12 (the shortest). Begin with a 7 or 8.

Quilting thread, heavier and stronger than sewing thread, is available in a variety of colors.

Start in the middle of your quilt and quilt toward the edges.
1. Thread your needle with 18" of thread and make a small knot at one end. Insert the needle into the quilt ½" from the desired starting point. Do not push the needle through, but stop it in the batting.
2. Bring the needle up through the top at your starting point. Tug gently on the thread to pop the knot through the top into the batting. This anchors the thread without an unsightly knot on the back.
3. With your non-sewing hand under the quilt, insert the needle with the point straight down in the quilt ¹⁄₁₆" from the starting point. With your underneath finger, feel for the point as it comes through the backing (Diagram 22).

continued

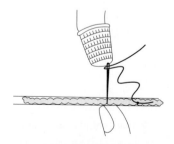

Diagram 22

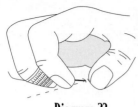

Diagram 23

4. Place the thumb of your sewing hand ½" ahead of the needle. When you feel the needle underneath, push the fabric up from below and rock the needle down to a horizontal position. Using the thumb of your sewing hand, pinch the fabric and push the needle back through the top **(Diagram 23)**.

5. Push the needle through to finish the stitch. Or reposition it to take another stitch. Take no more than 5 or 6 stitches before pulling the needle through.

6. When you have 6" of thread left, tie a knot in the thread on the surface of the fabric. Pop the knot through the top as you did before, and clip the thread.

Making Continuous Binding

A continuous bias strip is most often used for binding, though a straight-grain strip can also be used. Bias is necessary when working with a scalloped edge to wrap nicely around the curves.

1. Start with the square of fabric specified in the instructions. Cut the square in half diagonally.

2. With right sides facing, join triangles **(Diagram 24)**. Press seam allowance open.

3. Mark off parallel lines, 2½" apart **(Diagram 25)**.

4. With right sides facing, align edges marked Seam 2, matching marked lines. Then offset the

lines by one marked width so that one edge is higher than the other as shown **(Diagram 26)**. Stitch seam.

5. Cut a continuous strip, starting at the point and following marked lines around the tube.

6. Press strip in half lengthwise, wrong sides facing.

Attaching Binding

1. Baste the quilt layers together ¼" from the edge. Trim backing and batting even with the quilt.

2. Pin binding to the quilt with raw edges aligned.

3. Leave a 4" tail of binding where you begin. Start with a backstitch and sew the binding to one edge of the quilt, sewing through all layers with a ¼" seam. Stop ¼" from the corner and backstitch **(Diagram 27)**.

4. Remove quilt from machine. Fold binding strip straight up, away from the corner, and make a 45°-angle fold **(Diagram 28)**.

5. Holding the fold in place, lay the rest of the strip down, aligning it with the next quilt edge.

6. Insert a pin from the back of the quilt at the end of your stitching line **(Diagram 29)**. Start sewing where the pin comes up **(Diagram 30)**.

7. Stitch around all sides. Stop about 4" before the starting point.

8. Bring binding ends together and hand-baste where they meet **(Diagram 31)**. Check seam; then machine-sew. Trim seam allowance and press open. Sew remaining binding to quilt.

9. Fold the binding to the back. At corners, press down one side first; then fold the other side over **(Diagram 32)**. Slipstitch the binding to the backing by hand.

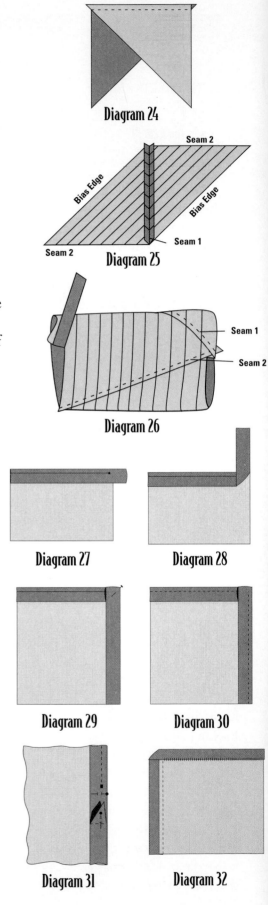

Diagram 24

Diagram 25

Diagram 26

Diagram 27

Diagram 28

Diagram 29

Diagram 30

Diagram 31

Diagram 32